Our Golden Age
Kaleidoscope

Our Golden Age
Kaleidoscope

COLLECTED MEMORIES
OF POST WWII YEARS

Compiled by **Ed Nef**

Ed Nef
601 North Fairfax Street, Unit 507
Alexandria, VA 22314

Printed in the United States of America

First Printing, 2020

ISBN print: 978-1-7341716-2-4
ISBN e-book: 978-1-7341716-3-1

Library of Congress Control Number: 2020905012

PHOTOGRAPHY CREDITS
Frontispiece photograph: Detail from "Agony of War" by PFC L. Paul Epley, of the 173 Airborne, 1966. Courtesy of the National Archives and Records Administration, Records of the Office of the Chief Signal Officer (111-SC-635974).

Photographs accompanying each chapter come from the contributors' personal collections. All rights reserved.

Book design by K. M. Weber, www.ilibribookdesign.com

Dedicated to my family—wife Elizabeth, daughters Christine, Patricia, and Stefanie, and grandchildren Thomas and Andrew Striegl and Emily and Abigail Marik. You have made my life so much more fun and interesting. I treasure the good humor, serious dedication, and positive attitudes we all share.

Contents

Preface

As our world seems evermore in turmoil, with old assumptions about normal behavior fading quickly and new assumptions arising with helter-skelter confusion, many of my generation look back upon the world we lived in around the middle of the twentieth century as a moment of critical importance for mankind. The 1950s saw the end of a horrific world war; the victors (we and our allies) helped the losers as they struggled to rebuild.

Post-war optimism had hardly taken its first breath when it began to collapse. New and unexpected wars suddenly popped up. It was our responsibility, the new generation, to make the new world work, the world we had inherited through no fault of our own. Everywhere we looked we saw looming threats, but also much promise. Our generation was optimistic: We would overcome difficulties; we would prevail. We also saw that unless these difficulties were resolved, the future could be ominous. A lot rested on our shoulders.

That generation, those who still survive, are now in their 70s and 80s. Well, that's us. We're surprisingly sprite and even still optimistic; we're a hell of a lot wiser, anyway. So how about this idea? What if we old guys and gals sat back and reminisced a bit? It seems like an interesting moment for us to write about that epoch—post-WWII and immersion in the Cold War. How did those years affect us? Do we have any good memories of those times? Were we oblivious to the implications of world events, or did we predict what was coming? Do we wish we had done anything differently?

There were no guidelines for our scribes as we took on this challenge; we wrote what we wanted about the era and about ourselves at that time. We wrote about disappointments, successes, and remarkable moments that we'll never forget. And, at our age, we did our best not to get cantankerous.

Those asked to participate were picked by me because I knew them to be nice people and fun to be with. They are intelligent, regular people who might lighten a reader's mind and have something interesting to say. A few are relatives on my Swiss side, living in Switzerland, who contribute a fascinating take on the post-war years. This book is a kaleidoscope, because each one of us experienced the same era from a unique perspective, and we came out of that time with different ideas, stories, and priorities.

Readers will no doubt find many common threads weaving through the essays in this book. I will highlight only a few. Military service looms large on these pages, some by draft and some by choice, but all indelible in our memories as a formative experience. Concern for international understanding and the world's environment feature prominently as well. Our experience with wars fuels our interest in peace; our appreciation for how the land used to look spurs our passion to keep it that way. In the end, despite our different paths and fortunes, we all turned out to be good-humored survivors.

The distinguished contributing authors are as follows:

Paul Doherty, former chair of the Boston College English Department and US Army veteran

George Proctor, former US Attorney, Department of Justice executive, immigration judge, and US Marine Corps veteran, Vietnam

Mike Dow, businessman, philanthropist, and US Army veteran

John Arnold, business executive and author

Gary Cunningham, retired airline pilot and US Marine Corps combat veteran, Vietnam

Doug Hartley, retired Foreign Service Officer, observer for the Organization for Security and Cooperation in Europe, and music director for Santis Productions

Robert Nef, master of law, former head of Liberales Institut in Zurich, and author

Maja Nef, retired school psychologist active in the women's movement in Switzerland

Erica Kuster-Nef, retired occupational therapist and managing director of the Swiss Association of Occupational Therapists, active in the women's movement in Switzerland

George S.K. Rider, former Wall Street trader, author, and US Navy veteran

William (Billy) Ming Sing Lee, retired architect and advocate of international friendship

Steve Young, professor of Northern Studies at Middlebury College and founder of the Center for Northern Studies in Vermont

Ed Nef, retired US government official (Foreign Service Officer, Senate aide, and Peace Corps manager), US Army veteran, school owner, film producer, and philanthropist

– Ed Nef

one

Soldier

by **Paul Doherty**

Paul Doherty, a native of Arlington, Massachusetts, served in the US Army, stationed just outside Stuttgart. Later he received his PhD in English from the University of Missouri and taught for forty-eight years in the Boston College English Department, serving two separate terms as its chair. In retirement he writes and reads, pulls weeds, and rakes leaves.

In the summer of 1957, following eight weeks of basic training at Fort Bliss, Texas, and then eight weeks of advanced training at Fort Gordon, Georgia, where I was trained to be a radio-teletype operator, I flew to Europe with a planeload of other soldiers in a noisy C-54, all of us sitting in metal bucket seats lining either side of the aircraft. Some, like myself, had been drafted and would serve a two-year obligation; others had enlisted for three or, in some cases, four years. We draftees tended to be older, college grads who had run out of deferments. Most of the enlisted soldiers were just a year or two out of high school; a few were high school dropouts. At twenty-four, I was an elder in the group.

The trip was in stages. The era of the jet plane lay just ahead, and prop planes like ours had to refuel halfway across the Atlantic at Gander International Airport, Newfoundland. From Gander we flew into Prestwick Air Base, near Glasgow, touching down on a fine, clear morning. My first picture of Great Britain was from the air; it was just as the poets had described it—tidy villages, small, enclosed fields, hedgerows, wooded copses, streams, and steep-banked winding roads. The next day we flew to Frankfurt, West Germany, where we boarded a troop train to Stuttgart, a few hours south. It was there, at Kelley Barracks in Moeringen, a tidy suburb of Stuttgart, that I would spend the next fifteen months, a member of the 34th Signal Battalion. West Germany had become, three years before, an independent nation, the Federal Republic of Germany. The post-war occupying forces of France, Great Britain, and the United States, which had governed West Germany since the end of WWII in 1945, had stayed in Germany, now as members of the newly formed North Atlantic Treaty Organization (NATO).

Kelley Barracks was a few miles southwest of Stuttgart, situated on a high plateau. It had been built just before WWII by the German military; its German name was Hellenen Kaserne.

It was renamed after the war by the US to honor Jonah E. Kelley, a posthumous Medal of Honor winner killed in the Battle of the Hürtgen Forest. It looked nothing like any American military base with which I was familiar. Those had rows of long, squat wooden barrack buildings, close together, dust and caked dirt all around. Everything hasty and temporary. At Kelley, the stucco, slate-roofed, two-story buildings fronted onto curved roads and were set apart from one another by grass and trees. Kelley was green. It was a model of planning, built to last.

When I arrived, I was not assigned to Company E with the other radio-teletype operators, but to Headquarters Company, where I replaced the company clerk who was soon to return to the US for discharge. That I never got to be a radio-teletype operator was no great loss for the Army, for I was neither a fast nor reliable typist, and, despite weeks of drills at Fort Gordon, my accuracy in sending and receiving Morse code was shaky.

My new job suited me better. My main duty, my sole regular duty, in fact, was to type the Morning Report. The Morning Report was a document, compiled daily—Sunday's typed on Monday—that listed all of the battalion's personnel activities for the previous day: arrivals, departures, leaves, promotions, demotions, temporary duty assignments, and AWOLs. Names, numbers, and abbreviations—that was the Morning Report. But a mystique of legend attached to it, for the Morning Report was believed to be, and perhaps was, potentially a legal document. I was pleased to participate in its aura, a bit of which shone on its preparer, as if I were in some way the agent of the news I chronicled.

There was, however, an unfortunate corollary of the legal presumption of the Morning Report. It had to be perfectly typed, no strikeovers. (The period of which I write was long before the dawn of Wite-Out, let alone the delete key and undo button.) If not perfectly typed, I was assured, the report would be useless as a legal document. It could not be introduced as evidence in a trial, and the government might thereby lose its case. Given my typing ability—so-so at best—preparation of the Report was a daily struggle. There would be many foul copies, crumpled and tossed into the wastebasket, before a fair one was produced. As my work for the day was pretty much over when the Report was cleanly typed, when I neared its end—so far so good—each word, each letter became an occasion for deliberation, concentration, and a deep breath, like a basketball player stepping up to the foul line with the game on the line. After the final accurate strike of a typewriter key, I carefully extracted the document from the cartridge of the Remington and walked down the cool, tiled hallway to the office of Chief Warrant Officer Haward A. Ryan who, after a quick once-over, signed it and sent me off to deliver this bit of military history to 7th Army Corps Headquarters, several buildings up the road.

"Good job, soldier."

"Thank you, sir."

After that I was free. The important thing now was not to be seen around the barracks looking idle, for there was always a danger of being summoned for a detail, a bit of temporary work, usually unpleasant, such as unloading a truck at the motor pool. I became expert at looking busy, killing as much time as I could without raising official suspicion.

Interruptions in this mild routine were infrequent. Guard duty once a month perhaps, and then a monthly "alert." The alert exercise went like this. Roused from sleep before daybreak by an alarm bell, we would jump into our fatigues, grab our mess kits, check out our rifles from the ordinance room in the basement, and pile into the HQ Company's 2.5-ton truck. It was a short drive to our field location, deep in a carefully groomed forest; the Jägermeister would wave us through the entrance. Under a canopy of tall pines, we would disembark, line up at the mess truck for breakfast and coffee, and report to the HQ tent set up by one of the other companies. There I would type up my Morning Report on a field typewriter. Except for the rude awakening, an alert was a pleasant diversion, over by noon.

The point of this exercise was to prepare for an invasion. Russian soldiers, in numbers and strength far surpassing our own, were stationed less than one hundred kilometers away on the Czech border, not far from the Danube, ready to invade Germany. Though this seems strange to me now, I don't recall having any preoccupation, let alone anxiety, about this possibility, a possibility which, in fact, was not at all remote. I have recently read that NATO intelligence at the time estimated it would not be prepared to defend Western Europe from Russian attack until 1967; in other words, nearly a decade after the scheduled end of my tour of duty in Germany. Ignorance is bliss.

I had more local concerns. One stands out. Gerry DiRienzo, soon to return to the States, anointed me to take over his highly prized job: ticket taking at the Kelley Barracks movie theatre. An honor. But one tradition of the new job, I soon learned, was that I was expected to allow Gerry and his friends from HQ Company to enter the movie house without paying for a ticket. They would present a ticket, the same ticket night after night, and, in a bit of sleight of hand, I was to pretend to take it from them. "Enjoy the show." An ethical dilemma. On the one hand, the eighth commandment, "Thou shalt not steal," is unambiguous; there's no wiggle room. On the other hand, this was pretty low-grade corruption—a ticket cost a quarter. Then there was the matter of barracks domesticity. Gerry and his friends had signed up for three or four years upon high school graduation; my set was drafted after college. The real social division needed to be bridged, not breached. Was this an appropriate occasion to appeal to a higher ethical standard, or to take into consideration the custom of the country? I had it both ways. At first I took the tickets presented by my incredulous barracks mates; later I reverted to the former practice and only pretended to take the offered tickets, adding confusion to incredulity.

Having taken (or not taken) the tickets, I was free to watch the movie, which I usually didn't, unless it was a Hollywood version of a classic novel that I thought would forward my interrupted literary education. Such a film I would watch over and over. *The Sun Also Rises*, *A Farewell to Arms*, and *The Brothers Karamazov* came to Kelley Barracks during the period of my employment. I saw each several times. My favorite was *The Sun Also Rises*, waiting for the end when Lady Brett Ashley (Ava Gardner) says to Jake Barnes (Tyrone Power), "Oh, Jake, we could have had such a damned good time together," and he answers, "Yes. Isn't it pretty to think so?"

Mostly, I took every opportunity to get off post, and opportunities abounded now that the occupation was over and the US and West Germany were cooperating members of NATO. Stuttgart was just a few miles away at the foot of a long winding hill, and just a few hundred yards from the main gate, at the end of a path through a field, was the trolley stop. The city had been 60 percent destroyed during WWII. It was a strategic target, an automotive city—Mercedes Benz and Porsche were located there—and toward the end of the war the city was indiscriminately bombed, purportedly to weaken the German resistance as in the earlier carpet bombings of Hamburg and Dresden. Even by my time, 1957, there were still areas of rubble, but rebuilding was going on rapidly. It was a busy and orderly city, booming in fact. The Marshall Plan and the World Bank had been major forces in restoring the West German economy. In the east, Russia, burdened by its great losses in World War II, was draining East Germany of resources in order to meet its own needs.

With John Ardoin and Robert Ray, I took German lessons at the Berlitz *schule* in downtown Stuttgart. The Berlitz method was to use only the language being learned. Herr Furster, a slight and serious man, began by holding up a blue pencil. "*Ein bleistift.*" We repeated, "*Ein bleistift.*" "*Ein blau bleistift.*" We repeated that. A second pencil. "*Zwei bleistiften.*" Then, "*Ein grün bleistift.*" And on through the *rot bleistift* and the *schwarz bleistift* and the *gelb bleistift*, and the *drei bleistiften* and the *vier bleistiften*, and the *fünf bleistiften, Und zu weiter.* We learned our colors and our numbers first, and in a very few lessons we were repeating, "*Wo ist der bahnhof?*" and later still, on our own now, "*Haben sie ein Zimmer frei für eine Nacht mit Frühstück, bitte?*" We were going places.

The three of us also attended performances of the Stuttgart State Opera. *Die Meistersinger* was the first opera that I had ever seen. Wagner was heavy; we saw the whole ring cycle together the next summer. Without Ardoin, I would never have ventured forth to opera. He was a tall, puffy Texan who had received a master of arts in music from Oklahoma University. His Army job was chaplain's assistant; this was even cushier than being Morning Report clerk. The chaplain's assistant was answerable only to Chaplain Mueller, and there appeared to be no telling when John would be needed to play or to practice the organ. No guard duty for a chaplain's assistant. Still, Army life was hard for John. He was gay. He was very untraditional in every way. He pretended that he wasn't in the Army. He called his footlocker his "box," his wall locker his "closet," his bunk (right above mine) his "bed." He lived for opera.

In later life, John became a quite famous music critic. His newspaper was the *Dallas Morning News.* I would hear him from time to time on Milton Cross's Texaco Opera Quiz during the Metropolitan Opera radio broadcasts on Saturday afternoons. He wrote several books about Maria Callas; they became friends. Perhaps twenty years after our Army sojourn, at a meeting of English teachers in Dallas, I went to a concert, hoping to see him there. See him I did at intermission, leaning against the bar rail. He acknowledged me only after I reminded him of our former association. He was not at all interested in touching up old memories of our months together in Germany and appeared to have suppressed most of that time in his life other than the operas; much, I suppose, as Dickens claimed to have no memory of that period in his life when his father's poverty required young Charles to work in a blacking factory. John died a few years ago; the *New York Times* obituary included his picture.

The third member of the Berlitz/opera group, Bob Ray, is someone I hoped to keep in touch with after Army days. He was the first African American person I had known. (There had been one African American student at Arlington High School during my years there; one at Holy Cross College during my years there.) I visited Bob at his home in Jersey City shortly after we had returned to civilian life, shortly before he went into permanent exile in Puerto Rico, where he managed a guesthouse in Santurce, San Juan. He sent one postcard with a picture of the guesthouse. I still have it. He did not answer my own letters. I believe—though I don't quite know the basis of my belief—that he left the United States because he had concluded that a life there as an African American was going to be too tough.

I used my leave time, all twenty-one days of it, to speed tour Europe. I preferred to be alone on my missions, following my whim of the moment, without plans except to keep moving. Nothing was quite so pleasant as taking a train for a new city, finding an inexpensive hotel with breakfast included, then walking around like Ben Franklin striding into Philadelphia with his loaf of bread. My goal was to set foot in as many countries as I could. Hit and run. It was possible to hitchhike rides on military planes if there was a vacant seat. "Hops" was the name for this practice. Hops got me to London and to Madrid. Sweden was a ferry ride from Copenhagen to Malmö and I could return on the same ferry a half hour or so later. Been there, done that. Lichtenstein was twenty minutes on a highway en route from Austria to Switzerland. Florence was a stopover between trains to Rome. To the galleries of the Uffizi and the Pitti I allotted a total of two and a half hours. On the way to the Brussels World's Fair, I passed through Luxembourg and crossed that little country off my must-visit list.

My guidebook, my text, was Arthur Frommer's *Europe on 5 Dollars a Day*. It told me what to see and how to see it for almost nothing. (Travel in Europe was very inexpensive at the time, but I was living on my Army salary.) In Rome, the USO found me a very inexpensive room with a bath in a private apartment. Too good to be true, I thought. I was right. The room was a bathroom; a gurney over the bathtub was the bed. *Macht nichts*, baths were a luxury in postwar Italy anyway. Trains were excellent for sleeping, killing two birds—movement and rest—with a single stone. And I remember a night boat trip from Strathearn in Scotland to Belfast. It was a very short sea voyage, no more than three hours, but you could board long before departure and have your night's sleep well underway before the boat left port. In London I stayed at the Sailors' Home. The layout was like that of a prison: two or three floors of sleeping quarters ringed an open central space. Guests were required to leave all their valuables at the front desk, where they were locked overnight for safety. I believe that the individual rooms had no doors, or perhaps it was that the doors had no locks. I'm not sure which. However, the hostelry was appropriately inexpensive. Many years later, I learned that an earlier guest had been the British seaman Józef Korzeniowski, who later Anglicized his name to Joseph Conrad.

By saving on lodging in London, I was able to see eleven plays in five days. This was possible because of a Saturday triple-header. The morning play was *Twelfth Night*. It was the first Shakespeare play I had ever seen performed, and it was an eye-opener. The audience, mostly schoolchildren and their teachers, drowned out the words with their glee at the antics of Sir Toby, Sir Andrew, and Maria. I didn't know that Shakespeare could be that funny. Later that day, the matinee audience for *My Fair Lady* at Covent

Garden included Winston Churchill and his wife. Like most others, I waited afterward to see them leave by the stage door. Winston and Clementine. We all clapped.

Other destinations were closer. You could, with a weekend pass, leave Kelley Barracks after Saturday inspection, which was usually over by late morning, and not return until Monday morning roll call. Two friends from Company E and Headquarters Company, Ed Nef and Mike Dow, had bought Austin-Healey sports cars. Ed would often take me along on overnight ventures; the Brussels World's Fair was one. We went to Oktoberfest in Munich. We skied Davos, Garmisch, and Saint Anton. I did not know how to ski and had no interest in learning, quite content to snowplow down the beginners' slope. *"Achtung! Achtung!"* little Austrian boys and girls would warn as they sped past. Summer was softball. I played second base on the Kelley Barracks team; this involved overnight trips to various tournaments. Another trip was to a weekend religious retreat at Berchtesgaden in the Bavarian Alps, once Hitler's getaway aerie.

—

In December 1958, when my two-year service requirement was near its end, Sergeant Stallings of Company A called me to his office. It fell to him to speak to each of us just before we returned to the States for discharge, regarding the benefits of reenlisting in the Army. I was ready for his spiel; some of my friends had already heard it. It was, of course, unimaginable that any of us would spend one day more than necessary, let alone three years more, in the United States Army. We were going places, weren't we? But the speech was part of Sergeant Stallings's job, something he had to do if only for the record.

When we met, the sergeant began with an apology. He said that he was sorry to be wasting my time. "Sorry to be wasting my time." This awkward preamble to what I suppose was the

standard reenlistment speech—I don't remember a word of it—
has stayed with me through the years. I suppose, though I cannot
be sure, that what it suggested to me at the time was the distance
between the sergeant's life and my own. Sergeant Stallings was
one of a group of 34th Signal Corps soldiers, NCOs, and warrant
officers whose careers had followed a similar trajectory. They had
served in WWII, had been recalled to duty for the Korean War,
and then, having spent so many years in the military already, had
decided to remain there until retirement. Considered individually they were decent men, fine men, but their common profile,
which they accepted and even contributed to, was unflattering.
Their profile, as I imagined it at that time, was this: In return for
food, shelter, steady work, generous allowances for their dependents, and attractive retirement benefits, these "lifers," as they
often referred to themselves, agreed to put up with whatever the
military had in store for them. This profile I accepted as truth.

Though I did not realize it then, Sergeant Stallings was not
wasting my time. It has taken a while, but I have come to think
of these career soldiers like Sergeant Stallings differently, with
a kind of admiration and even affection. To put it simply, their
military careers had been more serious than my own. They had
been tested in a way that I had not been and would not be. They
had had occasions to demonstrate courage, that ancient male
virtue. Some, like Jonah E. Kelley, didn't make it. Those who did
survive those occasions well deserved the care and protection the
United States government later provided them. As my period
of military service fell safely between the Korean and Vietnam
wars—peacetime—I had missed those occasions, and you can
be very sure I have not missed missing them.

But that is not exactly true, for sometimes I surprise myself
wondering what kind of soldier I might have been if I had been
put to the test. Would I have been brave? Would I have been a
coward? Would I have looked out for my buddies, or only for
myself? Would I have been something in-between? I'll never

know. Now on TV I watch American soldiers on dangerous missions in the Middle East. I try to put myself in their shoes, but it is impossible. You have to have been there. And I haven't been there; and I haven't done that. That is what I know now, but I also know that from time to time I have felt this untested courage in my life—whether its presence or its absence I cannot know—felt it as an amputee might feel a sharp pain where the missing limb once was.

———

One final piece of good luck at the end of my service career. On the troopship USS *Geiger*, bound from Bremerhaven, West Germany, to the port of New York, I was assigned to the officers' and dependents' library. I had the run of the upper decks, while the rest of the draftees and enlisted men were crammed below. On the morning of the sixth day out, we entered New York harbor. It was before dawn, so I did not get to see the Statue of Liberty waiting for me.

After mustering out at Fort Dix, New Jersey, I was back home in Arlington. On my first civilian day I slept until early afternoon. Then, slipping my skates onto the crook of my hockey stick, and nestling that against my right shoulder, I walked down to Hills Pond, a mile or so away. There was a pickup hockey game in progress. Teddy Stewart saw me skating idly on the verge of the action. "Long time no see," he said, and got me into the game.

Two

Outside My
Comfort Zone

by **George W. Proctor**

*George served in Vietnam as a US Marine officer. After nine years of
private law practice in Arkansas and a two-year term in the legislature, he was appointed United States attorney by Presidents Carter
and Reagan, and confirmed by the Senate. George prosecuted public
corruption cases on Saipan, CNMI, and worked as a senior executive officer in the Department of Justice in Washington, DC. He
served as an immigration judge in Los Angeles and San Francisco.*

On a hot, humid autumn Friday night in 1958, a perfectly spiraled football sailed over my left shoulder into my hands as I eyed the goal some twenty yards away. Seventeen years earlier, seven months before Pearl Harbor, I was born in a 1,000-square-foot home in Cotton Plant, Arkansas, population 1,600. Twelve years earlier, when I was five, my father had succumbed to a heart attack, leaving my two sisters and me to the care and support of our mom, a housewife.

Among the fans attending our game were those who remembered my father's exploits on this same field and, later, on a college field. Trophies evidencing my father and his brother's success in football and track were prominently displayed in the lobby of the school auditorium. Perhaps to meet the expectations that I could follow in my father's footsteps, I joined the senior high football team as a freshman—the only freshman to do so—too young to play in games but eager to prepare for the coming three years of eligibility. Those who had seen my father play or heard of his talent were surely disappointed with this 2.0 version of George Washington Proctor Jr. Though by my senior year I was some four inches taller, at 6 feet 3 inches, and thirty pounds heavier, at 187, than my father, and I could finish first in the 100, even running against the backs, I didn't enjoy hitting other boys. Not so my father. When professional boxers came to Cotton Plant to take on the local champ, they had to take on my dad.

Our coach did appoint me co-captain and later "Best All-Around Athlete"—more for my perseverance and athleticism than for my performance. He was so desperate to make me more aggressive he once said he would feed me raw meat if it would make me meaner. When I made a hard tackle on Gillette's star halfback, incredulous regular fans lining the field would not believe it was me. In a tackling drill I once tackled one of my best friends with so much force I felt guilty, and I never hit with such drive again, except on the tackling dummy. Hitting dummies was fun; hitting players not so much.

My assignment on defense was to defend left end and force running backs inward. I just had to look as big and menacing as possible to carry out the plan. Most of the opposing running backs were half my size. With shoulder pads and my large frame, I thought I looked pretty good. But for the game when I caught the pass, I wanted to look really good. So I bought knee-length socks like I'd seen on the University of Arkansas Razorbacks. Unlike the socks I had seen on college players, mine were all cotton—no elastic to hold them up once I'd sweated into them. And apparently sweat I did, as they sagged. As the goal line lay clearly within reach, with the ball held firmly in my hands, I planted a cleat of my shoe into the sagging sock and stumbled to the ground, face down, spread-eagle, some ten yards from pay dirt. To this day, I have a scar on my shin from the cleat to remind me of perhaps the dumbest thing I'd done at that point in my life. In a small town, you're known for the dumbest thing you've ever done.

I remember little of my father's death, though the stress level in our family must have been off the charts: a single mom with three children, mourning the love of her life. The two years or so before my mother married my stepfather are a blur, though I do recall being AWOL from the first day of kindergarten. I left a few minutes after my mom thought she'd dropped me off for the day. I didn't like what I saw there.

Though our stepfather was really our father, we could not bring ourselves, so soon after our dad's death, to call him "Dad." "Mr. James" was no good either. We decided on "Daddy Johnny." Handsome, ambitious, warm, a deacon in the church, he loved us as his own. He was quite a catch. And did I mention he owned the movie theater? We won the lottery! I still remember asking my mom whether we'd have to pay the nickel to see a movie.

Daddy Johnny built an addition to his nice brick home to accommodate my sisters and me. The four-bedroom, two-bath home with pantry and hallway dissecting the house was one of the nicest in Cotton Plant. And, according to my mom's wishes, Daddy Johnny sold my father's liquor store. Later he acquired the local insurance business. Ultimately, he parlayed political connections into an appointment as postmaster. But his greatest contribution to our family was a baby sister, twelve years my junior. Martha Lola from age two performed from a table at the local cafe. She sang, she danced, and she charmed all the customers to the great pride of Daddy Johnny. I had such love and respect for him that I discussed with my mom changing my name from my dad's to James. She rejected it out of hand, as did Daddy Johnny.

Next to football, hunting and the Boy Scouts were major parts of my life. I was proud of being awarded merit badges for marksmanship and other skills, just two short of Eagle Scout. Unfortunately, before I had a chance to earn those, the Boy Scouts' home office jerked our charter as punishment after some of our more adventurous scouts burglarized a farmhouse. Ironically, the two badges I lacked were physical fitness and religion—even then I was a fitness nut, and much of my social life revolved around our Methodist church where my mother played the organ. Speaking of my mom, if Cotton Plant had a saint, she was it. No one was more beloved than she.

Along with my father and his father, I am a George Washington, and all the name entails. Like George Washington, I could not tell a lie—that's right, "could not," not "cannot." (My mother, on the other hand, could not tell a lie in the George Washington sense.) While a teenager, my buddies and I needed change for a Coke. Because we knew the clerk at the drug store would not give change except in connection with a purchase, I was chosen by a flip of a coin with my buddies to purchase a stick of gum in order to obtain the change we needed to get three Cokes. We had enough for only one. But I was caught off guard when, after offering my dollar to the clerk, he asked if I didn't have smaller change. Blushing (as I do to this day), I said yes and tendered my nickel. As I write this, I'm tempted to say my conscience governed my actions, but in all candor, I feared I could not pull it off. Among other things, my bright red blush would have given me away.

Though Cotton Plant was a majority black town, no blacks held elected office, and none were welcome in white restaurants, churches, or the movie theater unless they were willing to sit in the balcony. The US Supreme Court in its 1954 landmark case of Brown v. Board of Education ordered the desegregation of schools. In my junior year of high school, Central High in Little Rock (from which my sons later graduated) was closed rather than comply. Black veterans of WWII were returning to face few job opportunities and attitudes that emasculated. Some fought back. Some were assaulted, jailed, and even lynched.

I would not have had contact with blacks, with the exception of our maid, had I not held a variety of jobs with them. I worked on Saturday nights behind the meat counter at a grocery store that catered to blacks, substituted for the black janitor of our theater, sold confectionary items to blacks attending the movies, and worked at the local veneer mill alongside blacks. Ironically, during the fifties, black culture was coming into its own, albeit sometimes through whites such as Elvis, Jerry Lee Lewis (who played the Augusta, Arkansas, prom) and Conway Twitty (who played my prom).

Our best athlete not only played basketball with blacks on a hoop out on his farm, but he adopted black dialect. He was elected most popular, more for what he brought as a conduit to black culture, particularly the vernacular. Today, it's deemed appropriation; then it was simply cool—the culture, not the individual black person.

In the spring of 1961 at the University of Arkansas, while dumping the garbage from the women's dorm where I washed dishes, dressed in a soiled T-shirt (think Ed Norton of *The Honeymooners*), unbeknownst to me, my future wife was checking me out. Still, she agreed to a blind (for me) date. We clicked, me driving her around aimlessly, realizing when I drove over a dirt road that I was in love. I admit to not having my mind on where I was going, and by no means was I driving to a secluded park for necking—it was many weeks (seemed like eternity) before we finally did. To my delight, Judy accepted my Sigma Chi pin and even wore it. Though many equate the pinning ceremony with a lite-engagement, I had passed mine around for the two years before I met her. In fact, when we needed the money and I sold it, I had to take bottom dollar—the clasp had suffered from the wear of the many coeds to whom it had been loaned.

When the time came and we were about to graduate, some fifty-six years ago, we married. Her friends, with good cause, said, "Proctor and Gamble." Judy was (and is) beautiful, intelligent, and vivacious, an A student in science, math, and literature. And I was, well, still adjusting to life beyond Cotton Plant and pulling down minimum requirements to graduate.

In the years leading up to the eighties, scholarship, beauty, and talent competitions were available to women; the professions—save teaching and nursing—were reserved for men. Judy's performance as an undergraduate would have placed her in the top rung of students in law or medical school. But had she attended either she would have been among only one or two other females in her freshman class. Fast forward to the early eighties: She graduated from law school with honors in a class with a majority of females.

We graduated from the University of Arkansas, a four-year college, as I must constantly remind my Ivy League friends. We affectionately referred to it as "The University"—for Arkansas, it was. My commission as a second lieutenant in the US Marine

Corps in the sixties was made possible by my graduation and completion of Platoon Leaders Class in two summers during college. Law school and admission to the bar were followed by solo law practice in the seventies, my career as a US attorney and manager of federal prosecutors in the eighties, my international responsibilities in the nineties, and, finally, my time on the bench as an immigration judge in the early twenty-first century.

My underachieving performance as an undergraduate in an admittedly unimpressive institution could've derailed a successful career. Call it male privilege, white privilege, or whatever, but I realize had I been faced with competition from females—not to mention people of color—my career might never have gotten off the ground. I would like to think given the added competition I would have worked harder and still succeeded, but who knows. As it was, when it came to academics, I subscribed to the attitude of the character created by *Mad Magazine*, "What, me worry?"

Before I was #woke (as my grandchildren say), I was comfortably ensconced in the role of male—law student, provider, king of the castle, master of my home, and much too important for mundane household chores and the raising of children. What could go wrong? I'm not positive as to when that changed, but I think it was on one hot day in the sixties in Fayetteville, site of The University, where I was a law student and Judy worked as a medical secretary for the VA hospital. We were juggling (okay, Judy was juggling) the care of our two young boys with the responsibility for the maintenance of a thirty-unit apartment complex. In return for our labor, we were provided an apartment rent-free. I was schmoozing with our boss, Jack, both of us with beers in hand, when Judy approached us carrying a bucket of water she had used to clean toilets. I saw Jack's jaw drop and his eyes widen, and when I turned to see why, I saw Judy, with strength I had no idea she possessed, throw the bucket into the air with water going everywhere. By the time the bucket hit the ground, I knew the game had changed.

Current literature is replete with theories explaining the role comfort zones play in our pursuit of happiness. Not so much has been written about that feeling you get when you're so far outside your comfort zone that you become fearful. You could say that when I committed to football, worked on pipelines for two summers in Iowa and Michigan, joined the US Marine Corps' platoon leaders' officer candidate school, or explored the interior of a ship at a depth of 140 feet scuba diving, I went outside most folks' comfort zone. Not mine; I had confidence in my athletic abilities, and none of those was a stretch.

On the contrary, I had no confidence in academics. Hence I was surprised (as was the Marine Corps) when my results from the general classification test placed my intelligence quotient higher than my fellow Marines' who had bested me in tests on such topics as the operation of the M14 rifle—boring. As a result of my performance on the test, I was assigned study to become an aviation supply officer. The others, for the most part, were assigned to platoons in Vietnam. This was a far cry from my wish to become a pilot (I was too tall for the Marine Corps' combat support aircraft) or an air delivery officer, which would mean jump school (there were no openings). I never considered becoming a platoon leader, which, with no war in sight at the time meant to me running around in the boondocks shooting blanks, playing Marine at war. Unlike most of my fellow Basic School classmates, I was married and soon to be a father.

Like many of my fellow officer candidates, I was inspired to be a Marine by all the movies glamorizing the Marines in the Pacific campaign in WWII. I read everything I could find that related to the region or the campaign, including James Mitchener's *Tales of the South Pacific*. Even the movie based on that book grabbed me. However, after I survived platoon leader's training and was commissioned as a second lieutenant, I found that Joseph Heller's book *Catch-22*, more than any of my other reads, captured the essence of serving in the US Armed Forces. Likewise, the essence of military service is demonstrated in the hilarious encounters of the more recent *M*A*S*H* TV series based on the 1968 novel of the same name.

While we were still in Basic School at Quantico, Virginia, we were told that the Army's Special Forces were taking on the North Vietnamese Communists. Cambodian, Vietnamese, and other Southeast Asians who trained with us in Basic School struggled to carry a rifle, rucksack, and other equipment we believed necessary to engage the enemy. Thus we were confident that the Vietnam conflict, if one could even call it that, would be short-lived. Years after the war I was privileged to talk with former Viet Cong of our mutual experiences. They explained that they traveled light, relying on a bag of rice for sustenance and water from streams, left with only a weapon for significant weight.

I had orders out of Basic School to Japan, but after under two months there we boarded an LST (landing ship, tank) destined for Vietnam. As in a favorite flick, *Sands of Iwo Jima*, I was John Wayne heading for the shores of a country (not an island, but close enough) in the Pacific. During two weeks at sea, unaware for security reasons of our landing site, we listened to the North Vietnam's propaganda arm spout threats from the likes of a woman who went by "Hanoi Hanna." No concerns there—Tokyo Rose had made similar threats and dire predictions for the greatest generation's Pacific campaign, and we know how that turned out.

We landed with no organized opposition. There were a few potshots, but they were likely from disgruntled farmers who didn't know what the hell was going on. We set up pup tents and later upgraded to general purpose tents housing a dozen or so Marines in each. Though John Wayne made no appearances, I once eyed Robert Mitchum saddled up to our officer's club bar drinking a beer, playing himself.

My year there was largely uneventful, with the exception of one night when incoming mortars had us diving into our foxholes dug beside our cots. The mortars, or possibly grenades—not sure

George Proctor in Chu Lai, Vietnam, 1965.

which—struck only yards away. I shudder today over the fear that gripped me. Never being able to sleep with my wedding ring, I had placed it on an ammo box beside my cot. In my haste to jump into my foxhole, I knocked the ring into the sand, where it was buried out of sight. Had I not been able to find it, my sweet Judy would have murdered me!

We were part of a Marine Expeditionary Force tasked with supporting an airstrip that the Seabees had hastily constructed with planking composed of a lightweight metal alloy. The strip was hardly longer than the deck of an aircraft carrier and required a catapult to launch planes and arresting gear to keep them from going off the strip into the jungle on landing. In little more than a month, an A-4 jet made the first landing on our strip. Our base was located on a beach so that should it come to it, we could evacuate via the South China Sea—the Viet Cong had no navy.

Our unit was assigned the obligatory physician, dentist, and clergy. Our dentist and clergy were not remarkable, though they drank too much (but that was the norm among those who weren't crucial to the mission). Those of us who were crucial to the mission worked seven days a week.

Our physician, a psychiatrist, was a character straight out of *M*A*S*H*. Though he didn't resort to dressing in drag, he deliberately wore his cap askance, responded to salutes from his corpsmen dismissively with Heil Hitler extended-arm salutes, and worked assiduously at being reassigned to our former base in Japan, realizing that getting back to the States was more than even he could accomplish. Once, when our commanding officer (CO) asked him why he had brought a suitcase to our daily meeting, he replied that when the CO ordered him back to Japan, he intended to be ready.

While we sweated it out in a war that was not going as planned, the doctor was eventually reassigned to air conditioning in Japan. He missed the night we slept outside our tents when intelligence warned that the Viet Cong would target our tent housing officers in an attack. And there was the time we assumed positions with weapons locked and loaded when the Viet Cong broke through our heavily guarded perimeter. (Why the Marine Corps trained all officers in the tactics and execution of the mission of a rifle platoon became obvious.) But like our psychiatrist, I was absent during a major infiltration of Viet Cong, on R & R, enjoying the air-conditioned comfort of a room in Hong Kong's Presidential Hotel.

Sad to say, but service in Vietnam presents a panoply of duplicity. We set sail from Japan to Vietnam in violation of the treaty prohibiting our deployment from Japan for hostile purposes. We were instructed to order our troops, if asked, to say that we had deployed from Okinawa (this preceded Okinawa becoming a Prefecture of Japan). To support the lie, we spent a night anchored off Okinawa Island. Many otherwise honorable participants in the Vietnam War found themselves a part of a larger lie. Most of the lies were above my pay grade as a first lieutenant. Assigned to teach my unit the topic of why we were in Vietnam, I became passive aggressive, merely letting it slide. Truth is, I didn't have a clue. In one of my letters home, I told my mother I was in charge of an excursion into the village to give the troops a taste of the local culture. Southern Vietnamese were not our enemy; that concept became less clear as the war progressed.

Charged with keeping track of some 300 Korean War surplus arctic sleeping bags, I failed to write them off according to Marine Corps regs. While they were inappropriate for the tropical conditions of Vietnam, Marines used them as cushion on their cots until they mildewed and were covered by mold. Then they were, in Marine Corps vernacular, "shit-canned."

But lo and behold, when our commanding officer had to account for the worthless sleeping bags, I became the fall guy. As a consequence, in spite of otherwise glowing fitness reports, I was punished by a letter in my file. So when most of my contemporaries were promoted to captain, I continued wearing the silver bars of a first lieutenant. And that ended the "What, me worry?" phase of my life. I attribute the success I enjoyed for the remainder of my career to the fact that I clearly drove myself beyond my comfort zone.

My orders out of Vietnam were to Norfolk, Virginia. When I wrote Judy, she wrote back that she had a contact through one of her bosses in the Equal Employment Opportunity Commission, where she worked, who might get my orders changed to DC. I scoffed at the idea—"That's not how it works," I wrote dismissively. Before she received my letter, my orders for Norfolk were superseded with orders to Arlington, Virginia. I left Vietnam aboard a C-130 cargo plane, designed for a quick ascent to avoid pesky Viet Cong taking potshots at the end of the runway.

On April 8, 1966, Judy and thirteen-month-old Chris greeted

me in the lobby of River House apartments in Arlington, Virginia. On January 8, 1967, our son Jason was born—nine months to the day from when I returned, count 'em.

In Arlington, I served as executive officer (EO) to a headquarters and service company. As the EO, I made periodic visits to Marines in Bethesda Naval Hospital who were administratively assigned to my unit. I'm still haunted by a redheaded seventeen-year-old quadriplegic. I participated in the ritual of burials at Arlington Cemetery, and, most difficult, I accompanied my commanding officer on casualty visits to parents and spouses of those killed in Vietnam. On the evening of the commencement of the Gulf War, a precursor to the 2003 invasion of Iraq, when we subjected Iraq to thousands of Tomahawk missiles and committed as many troops to battle, I suffered a heart attack. I don't think the invasion was the cause, though it had to have been a major factor in the timing.

Not until the nineties did I ever hear a "Thank you for your service." (I was never spat upon, but service in Vietnam was no badge of honor in the seventies or eighties.) The thank-you-for-your-service recitations I hear today evoke many emotions. First, I think of my contribution compared with those who made the ultimate sacrifice, whose missions resulted in injuries, physical as well as mental. Second, I suspect those speaking are assuaging their guilt over being part of the 99 percent failing to make the sacrifice. Most of all, I fear they feel they are fulfilling their sole debt to veterans, while supporting politicians who vote for endless wars yet fail to vote for benefits for the veterans who have made those wars possible. But, like most veterans, I acknowledge them with a nod of my head and volunteer that I did not have a combat mission (combat pay in a combat zone, yes, but no search and destroy for me).

As someone who grew up in rural Arkansas, my seed hardly germinated, much less bloomed, until my mid-twenties. Networking, largely unavailable to women before the eighties, propelled my career. My first mentor was Arkansas Supreme Court Judge George Rose Smith, for whom I clerked after law school. He suffered neither fools nor tedious oral arguments. He once pronounced that he had to refrain from coffee before "hearing" oral arguments, because the caffeine kept him awake.

Friends were surprised when I took a part-time position as a prosecutor for Woodruff County, Arkansas, where most defendants were in trouble by virtue of their poverty or race. Judy and I had our two boys, and I was a solo practitioner, so it was comforting to have a monthly check. But that was not the main reason I chose to prosecute. After all, even after my practice became lucrative and serving as prosecutor proved costly in that I had less time for paying clients, I chose to stay. Ours was tantamount to a feudal system, with power in white landowners to whom the sheriff owed allegiance. The prosecutor held immense power for good or evil.

The municipal judge had little use for the Constitution or a prosecutor who followed the law. He once complained to the elected prosecutor, several counties away, that I hindered him in his "enforcement" of the law. Though no great defender of the rule of law, my boss above all wanted to remain elected, and out of respect for my own political popularity, he allowed me to stay. Not the least of the complaints was one coming from our sheriff that I was a runner, often seen running aimlessly across the county before sunup. When he snitched on me to the elected prosecutor, the prosecutor became apoplectic, not thinking I was running for exercise, but in a political sense for office against him!

Though in high school I was uncomfortable in my speech class, I was in my element in the school play—I loved hamming it up. My stage became the municipal court, where we tried all the down and dirty misdemeanors, and it was the primary source of entertainment for the denizens of Woodruff County. A particularly flamboyant attorney from McCrory would play my antagonist, with equal billing, of course. Shamelessly we played to our audience, most of whom had been coming to municipal court before television, and this was before *Judge Judy* and other TV shows of that ilk. But we were mere novices as courtroom thespians when compared to my second mentor, Bill Wilson. Representing a fellow lawyer charged with driving under the influence, Bill, after exhausting all defenses, removed a white towel from his briefcase and threw it over to counsel's table, symbolically and literally throwing in the towel and conceding.

This was Woodruff County in 1970, eleven years after Central High had closed to avoid court-ordered integration, and friends were fleeing Cotton Plant to the surrounding towns where they could comfortably remain in the majority. Simply put, they feared blacks in the majority. For the first time in history, the remaining residents elected a black mayor with a majority black council. A former friend attempted to hire me to fight the black incursion in the schools and government. I declined, aligned myself with change I saw for the good, and became Cotton Plant's city attorney. To his credit, my stepfather, while living in Cotton Plant, lent to the fledgling council the institutional memory he had gained as a previous mayor.

Later, when the black school board hired a black superintendent, I became the school attorney. I remained loyal to my hometown, and not only with my legal services; when Augusta played Cotton Plant in basketball, Judy and I sat with the Cotton Plant fans. And, yes, as the only whites, we stood out.

Politics was ingrained in me early on—progressive politics, that is. Must have been in my DNA, as my sisters were likeminded. Adlai Stevenson was my man. He was among those who created the United Nations, he stood up to the Red Scare, and he was believed to have laid the groundwork for the election of John F. Kennedy. Then there was Hubert Humphrey and a long line of liberal losers of the popular vote, but winners in my heart, nevertheless. Not totally wedded to liberals, I also admired the pragmatists with actions that can only be described as profiles in courage: FDR, LBJ, and JFK. (That you recognize them by their initials speaks volumes of their contributions.) Still, until I took a political science course in my senior year of college, I did not realize that I would become a political junkie.

With college, Vietnam, law school, a clerkship, and two years solo law practice in the seat of the county I grew up in behind me, I filed for the Democratic nomination for state representative. When I asked my mother what she thought—she was, after all, the daughter of a former state senator on her father's side and the granddaughter of a former speaker of the house on her mother's side—she said, with a twinkle in her eye, that she'd likely vote for me if she found me to be the more qualified candidate. Though uniquely qualified for representative of our agriculturally based district, my rice farming opponent apparently did not win over my mother. When I only got 82 percent of the vote out of Cotton Plant, she became visibly angry at the 18 percent who voted for my opponent, who lived right outside Cotton Plant.

My district was one of the most conservative in the state. We were in the Mississippi River Delta, not in the state of Mississippi, but you get the picture. Upon my announcement that I would not seek reelection, a reporter wrote (presumably because of my support for a civil rights bill, unions, abolishing the death penalty, environmental preservation, criminal justice reform, and ratification of the ERA for women) that the House was losing a stalwart liberal—a death knell for political ambition in Arkansas.

While in the Arkansas legislature, I was designated to present arguably the most important legislation of our term. The other sponsors of our bill to protect and preserve wetlands from exploitation were far senior to me. In fact, one was speaker for the house. But I was the only lawyer, maybe the only college graduate. The night before my presentation, the oldest and longest-tenured legislator had the unfortunate experience of being mugged by a prostitute (his, in fact). He appeared for the hearing as a tragic figure with a black eye and his arm in a sling. With as much drama he could muster, he stood and announced that though he had intended to present the bill, due to the unfortunate circumstances of the previous evening, he had asked young Proctor to present it in his stead. Those legislators with thoughts of "But for the grace of God go I" (most of them) were in my pocket. The bill passed.

Conditions for women in Arkansas improved, but not enough for the ratification of the Equal Rights Act for women, which I championed as a representative in the Arkansas legislature in the early seventies. Of our hundred representatives, we had no more than a dozen female legislators. One of our senior male members was infamous for maintaining women should be kept barefoot and pregnant. And so went the rights of women in our state and the nation. On the other hand, while serving as US attorney and later as a senior executive in the Department of Justice, the majority of my lawyer hires were women—on merit.

Though my solo practice was successful, it lacked the challenge and opportunity to prosecute wrongdoing, particularly public corruption—my growing interest, fed by my stint in the legislature. As my law practice became more lucrative, I was feeling more like the character Gordon Gekko in *Wall Street* than my hero Atticus Finch in *To Kill A Mockingbird*.

US District Judge Billy Roy Wilson, an unabashed self-described liberal and my mentor during my time as a prosecutor in Woodruff County, is a close friend. He brokered with our senators my appointment as US attorney, a position I did not seek. I don't know what he would have said had I not jumped at the chance of being a US attorney after he had persuaded the senators I was their man. Perhaps he knew that I would have been a fool not to go for it. This catapulted me from a solo law practice in rural (my urban friends say that "rural" is redundant) Arkansas to the world stage (hyperbolic, perhaps, but that's the way I saw it then).

The most satisfying aspect of my career was my decade devoted to routing out public corruption as a US attorney. That and the fact that my two-year term in the legislature paralleled the corruption uncovered in Watergate were fodder for public corruption prosecutions. And what better way to prepare one for prosecuting public officials than to have walked in their shoes, facing on a daily basis the temptations that become irresistible for far too many? During my nine years as US attorney, we convicted seventeen county judges and the Little Rock city attorney for corruption, largely based on kickbacks for government purchases. Most went to trial, and I participated as lead attorney in them all. I personally tried three county judges in my second year in office.

I tried cases with an assistant US attorney, but I always reserved the cross-examination of the defendant judge for myself, thinking I could hit the hardest, striking a blow for justice and obtaining admissions which I would pound home on final argument. Future events belied my confidence. To my embarrassment, some of the imprisoned judges sent me Christmas cards, expressed no hard feelings, and described me as a gentleman, the prosecutor they would choose to conduct their cross-examination. That was not the reaction I sought. In retrospect, perhaps my inability to hit hard in football spilled over into my legal career. Still, we never lost a case. We were among the first to indict under RICO (the Racketeer Influenced and Corrupt Organizations Act). The juries shared our disgust with corruption and refused to tolerate it.

Ed Bethune, a former prosecutor for whom I prosecuted, was my third mentor. Ed is a highly respected former congressman and a former special agent of the FBI who was on the short list for director of the FBI. He was one of two Republicans in Arkansas who held an elected federal office in the state, and he was able to talk the Reagan White House (via Rudy Giuliani) into continuing me as US attorney after the Carter administration. My appointment was no small feat: of ninety-three US attorneys, only three of us were held on from the Carter administration. And I was the only one who remained a Democrat. Ed is my kind of Republican—fiscally conservative, socially tolerant, a free trader, and a steward of our environment—in these days, a rare breed.

In the early eighties, when my reappointment was very much up in the air, my fellow US attorneys (Republicans all) elected me as chair of the Attorney General's Advisory Committee, in essence, president of the US attorneys. This not only provided Ed with an argument for my retention, but it gave me a seat close to the new administration, working closely with Ken Starr, Rudy Giuliani, and Attorney General William French Smith. I was privy to unguarded conversations with Smith. On one occasion, noting his frustration with the National Rifle Association over their opposition to legislation enhancing punishment when a gun was involved, I asked him whether the NRA had not become a lobby for criminals, to which, surprisingly, he agreed.

Though public corruption prosecutions were my passion as US attorney, I steered my assistants toward white collar crime, along with some drug cases focusing on suppliers. I hired the top trial attorney out of the Department of Justice's civil rights section in DC and formed a civil rights section in my office. We met with limited success. I obtained an indictment against a Jonesboro police officer for assaulting a black man. The victim had a record, but most black men did for offenses for which whites often enjoyed immunity. A jury of whites acquitted the cop in about fifteen minutes. But we sent a message: The United States and a grand jury declared that the police officer was in violation of the law.

Though we had a relatively small US attorney office, with only some twenty-five employees, my press conferences announcing indictments of judges were at times covered in the national media. NBC interviewed me for an hour in my office for a two-minute clip in their morning show. One early morning, Martha called me from the East Coast to alert me that my interview was aired on NBC's *TODAY Show*—for me, heady stuff.

It was not until Bill Clinton was serving his first term as president that I found myself on the opinion pages of a national newspaper. The *Wall Street Journal* opined in two editorials that I'd given Clinton's brother, Roger, a sweet deal on cocaine distribution. In fact, that case against Roger was not even in my district. Rather, it was in the district of another US attorney, now governor of Arkansas. He was the one who (wisely, I think) gave Roger Clinton immunity in connection with bolstering an investigation in his district. The *Journal* criticized me as well for the plea deal we gave a junk-bond millionaire for providing cocaine gratis to young women as party treats. Under the agreement, he was sentenced to six months in prison. He had, however, contributed more to Governor Clinton's campaign than anyone else. So the *Journal* was suspicious. Ironically, the Arkansas papers were suspicious for the opposite reason: My aggressive prosecution of a friend of Clinton was attributed to my appointment by the Reagan administration. The Arkansas papers, although mistaken, based their claim of partisanship on arguable facts, where the *Wall Street Journal*'s opinion piece was based on poor reporting at best.

In my final year as US attorney, facing a questionable future in light of the increasing success of Republican office holders—I remained a Democrat—I read with interest a solicitation to all US attorney offices from the US attorney on Guam for a prosecutor with a public corruption mission for the island of Saipan, CNMI. The CNMI is a separate judicial district and a commonwealth of the US, but the only judicial district without a US attorney. Corruption was rampant, resulting in much of the financial aid provided by the US government ending up in the pockets of local elected officials. The FBI was stationed on Guam, because the CNMI was determined too dangerous.

I arrived on this Pacific island under the command of a former Marine, now US attorney on Guam, forty-three years to the month (July), when the Marines fought their way ashore in a victory, albeit with the loss of some 3,000 men. Was I still wrapped in the romance of the WWII Pacific campaign? Perhaps, though you'd think my Vietnam experience would have washed that from my system.

My acceptance of the position was mixed: Our chief judge in Arkansas was nonplussed (should I have told him first?), and the media was favorable except for one scribe who opined that I was choosing an idyllic island life, mentioning my scuba diving hobby, over Arkansas. The *Wall Street Journal* ran a story regarding my assignment to the CNMI on their front page (they had followed corruption in the CNMI). When I pointed this out to the Arkansas scribe, he conceded I'd gotten the last word.

But the reaction that rings in my ears came from a friend whose father had closely followed my career. He said, "Proctor's really screwed up this time. They're sending him to Saipan!" FBI screwups of the day were said to be exiled to Butte, Montana. My friend's father figured I'd messed up so badly this time, they were sending me halfway around the world.

At the urging of the FBI, I was deputized as a deputy US Marshal solely to enable me to carry a firearm. I had been threatened by people affected by my work as a federal prosecutor, and the FBI had deemed Saipan too dangerous to station their agents there. Though probably unrelated to our investigation, one witness was murdered execution-style while strolling the beach. I opted to go without a sidearm after reflection on my experiences in the Marine Corps and despite the advice of the fellow Marine veteran who was the US attorney on Guam.

When on Saipan, I had one of many feelings of "I'm not in Kansas anymore" when I presented a Japanese mega-corporation employee, accused of bribing a local official for permission to build a luxury hotel, with a standard offer I believed he could not refuse. I said in my best prosecutor voice, "It's you or your employer who takes the hit—you decide." He said, "You don't understand. Should my employer instruct me to commit suicide—*hari-kari*—I would be obliged to obey." Whoa. Thanks to my Saipan experience, by the time I represented the Department of Justice internationally, I had overcome much of my naivety.

Saipan also gave Judy and me a taste for living as a minority. We were identified in a bill from one restaurant on Saipan as "the *haole* couple." Of some 60,000 Saipan residents, all except about 2,000 Caucasians were Pacific Islanders or Asians.

The Department of Justice commemorated my fourth mentor, David Margolis, by naming the highest award available for a career employee after him. On Saipan, as I weighed a career with Justice against returning to Arkansas, David offered me a position as his deputy in the organized crime section of the criminal division. Though I had no experience prosecuting the mob, I was among the small fraternity of prosecutors who had actually charged and tried a RICO case—Justice's most effective charge of mobsters. In fact, I had tried many RICO cases.

As David's deputy, I supervised prosecutions of the mob in Miami, the northern district of New York, and New Orleans. I entered a world of organized crime, listening to wiretaps and other conversations of mob activities It was pure entertainment. In fact, many former prosecutors have become successful authors through information gleaned from wiretaps. Most memorable was the statement I overheard of a mob boss who, while conducting an induction of a "made guy," said, "If only these walls could talk." In fact, they did.

Later, after a year of managing the forfeiture office under Bob Mueller, who ran the Department of Justice's criminal division, he named me head of the international affairs office. I had some twenty-five lawyers and a like number of paralegals and clerks, with responsibility for all extraditions and renditions (obtaining fugitives through means other than via treaty) and the negotiation of mutual legal assistance treaties and exchanging evidence pursuant to those treaties. I had lawyers in Rome and Mexico City, but the others were in my office in DC.

It was not until the latter part of the eighties and those years

George attending the Taiwan Symposium
on Economic and Narcotics Crime, 1993.

following—Vietnam, Hong Kong on R&R, and Japan notwith-standing—that I was introduced to the world at large. Trips to Rome, Mexico City, Tokyo, Lisbon, Paris, Strasbourg, Lyon, Taiwan, Beijing, Hong Kong, Cayman Islands, Guatemala, Bo-gotá, El Salvador, and Cairo, to name a few, carrying the banner for the most respected law enforcement unit in the world, was quite an experience for a boy from Cotton Plant.

A highlight of my travels was sitting in the chair reserved for heads of state next to the president of Taiwan, discussing law enforcement. And then there was the drive through Tokyo with police escort. Police in Bogotá accompanied my party with arms locked and loaded as we negotiated with limited success the extradition of members of a drug cartel. My personal tour guide for our embassy in Paris was none other than Ambassador Pamela Harriman.

I chose to retire at fifty-seven because, to put it bluntly, I feared I was nearing my expiration date, and there was much I wanted to do. Of course, saying that twenty-one years later, in good health, sounds stupid. But I had suffered a heart attack seven years earlier, my father had succumbed to a heart attack at the tender age of thirty-five, and a cousin my age had died of a heart attack the year of my own heart attack. In retrospect, I did not take into account that I had led the life cardiologists promote: a jogger from my early twenties, including a marathon, weight control, a heart-healthy diet, tennis, rowing, swimming, you name it. When I retired, I could do twenty-five pull-ups and twice as many push-ups. I wasn't ready to die, but I didn't know that then.

Many have asked me how a boy from Cotton Plant ended up in San Francisco, which has been our home for the past fourteen years. It was a journey that began in Cotton Plant but proceeded through Fayetteville, Arkansas; Quantico, Virginia; Iwakuni, Japan; Chu Lai, Vietnam; Arlington, Virginia; Fayetteville (again); Little Rock, Arkansas; Augusta, Arkansas; Little Rock (again); Saipan, CNMI; Washington, DC; Santa Monica, California; and, finally, San Francisco. Early on, a friend called us "grasshoppers" for our constant moves. In fact, our time in San Francisco is the longest we've lived anywhere.

I returned to San Francisco for the first time since Treasure Island in the early nineties with a fellow US attorney, now governor of Arkansas. In route to a conference in Southern California, we drove down the coast from San Francisco. I was hooked. After six years in Santa Monica—four on the beach and two on the immigration bench in Los Angeles—I transferred to San Francisco to judge for three years before my second retirement. Los Angeles and Santa Monica had beach bums, agreeably diverse with their Latino culture, but all things revolved around the making of movies, cosmetic surgery, bodybuilding, and driving everywhere. San Francisco means tolerance, diversity (Asian, Latino, Indian), culture, walking, density, the bay—in short, paradise. Because we travel so much—three international trips thus far this year—some doubt our love for our hometown, but we have never enjoyed returning home as much as we have since living here.

Sitting as an immigration judge for five years in Los Angeles and San Francisco has made me even more appreciative of the contributions made by immigrants. Though politicians pander to the racism and paranoia of voters who fear immigrants, there's never been a truer cliché than that we owe our success to immigrants.

Today I revel in the fact that both our sons have chosen immigrant wives of color—one from Barbados and the other from the Philippines. Both of our daughters-in-law are proud, strong, intelligent women, one a physician and the other an office manager.

To make sense of the problems that face us today, I go back to the years between WWI and WWII, when the great FDR addressed fears brought about by the Depression with his famous pronouncement: "The only thing we have to fear is fear itself—nameless, unreasoning, unjustified terror which paralyzes needed efforts to convert retreat into advance."

Beginning with Cotton Plant, where it all started for me, fear has virtually destroyed my hometown. Today there are a mere 600 or so residents, mostly black. Friends there tell me no immigrant has chosen to live there, there is no longer a school of any sort, and as a sign of the times (for the US, but incongruous for my hometown), the only employer is a marijuana processing operation authorized by the state. However, it doesn't employ locals.

To be frank, notwithstanding my obsession in my teens with Marines storming the beaches and with the brave men of Normandy, I can't imagine the courage of those Marines and soldiers. But a reasonable hypothesis espoused by many is that, while they have a fear of dying, it is subordinated to the fear of letting down their fellow Marines and soldiers. I do believe that in Vietnam, Iraq, and Afghanistan, those who have fought even though they do not support the cause do so for their comrades in arms. On the topic of our military involvement in the Middle East, never has FDR's admonition of being governed by fear been more relevant. We developed an irrational fear after 9/11 and sacrificed fine young men and women, as well as our prestige, to an area of the world where we were unwanted and unneeded.

Not that long ago, I saw tottering WWII vets. Now we Vietnam vets are the ones limping around on canes and walkers and, regrettably, most of the vets of WWII have died. By conceding that I'm offended when a middle-aged woman offers me her seat on the bus, can I claim that I am aging gracefully? Probably not. Still, ironically, the fear I had in my fifties of death at age seventy-eight is long gone. Death is inevitable, but only a tragedy for those who have been denied a full life by an early death. Not for me. While I would miss watching my sons and grandchildren continue to flourish and while leaving the love of my life is unthinkable, I'm ready.

A friend described my life as "serendipitous." I can't quarrel with that. Virtually every step of the way has been guided by good fortune. Perhaps because I have been lucky, I expect things to turn out for the better, and they always have. We all owe a great debt to those young soldiers who lost their lives at Normandy and the Marines who died in our Pacific campaign, most before they could experience the joy of family, career, and the many opportunities offered us as Americans. And even more regrettable is the loss of life in the unfortunate conflicts of Korea, Vietnam, Iraq, Afghanistan, and Syria. For those of us who have led fruitful, complete lives, we owe much to these heroes. I often think of my father, who died at such a young age, and of my cousin, who died at age fifty. It really has been a good run, and, hey, may it continue!

Three

Honesty, Humility, and Enthusiasm

by **Mike Dow**

Mike was born in Michigan in 1935 and served in the US Army from 1956 to 1958, stationed in Stuttgart, Germany. He graduated from Michigan State University in Mechanical Engineering in 1961. Mike began his career working with several partners to create a mini-conglomerate of newspapers, FM radio stations, and a TV station. He invested in and built several Holiday Inn hotels, a condo marina, a marina business, an aircraft business serving private aircraft, and an aircraft manufacturing company building and selling a replica of a 1935 open cockpit biplane. He is currently active on several local nonprofit boards in northern Michigan as

well as family-related private foundations. Mike has been married to his wife, Rhea, since 1960, and they have two children and four grandchildren.

After World War II, life settled down for me and my family as I grew up through high school in Midland, Michigan. That meant breakfast and dinner in our dining room with Mom and Dad and my two younger sisters. My father was already a successful architect, and we had completed our family's move into an amazing new home with his attached architectural office, all designed by him in the Frank Lloyd Wright style. To me, it was just home. But to my friends and others, it was an amazing architectural masterpiece!

Those family dinners together often featured conversations about something interesting that had happened to Dad that day. Once he said, "I had the most wonderful drive today on that brand-new highway heading north. It wound around this way and that in such a pleasing way. It was wonderful!" Another day he would describe the new construction of a church that excited him. He always found something new and exciting.

An item of philosophy he wound into conversation was his belief in honesty, humility, and enthusiasm, known to us kids as "HH&E." A building should be honest, have humility, and exude enthusiasm. He would use the same HH&E test for most any idea, even for the construction of that new highway.

Our little city of Midland became an amazing collection of mid-century modern structures: sixty-three homes designed in that medium by my dad, and ultimately 284 similar homes designed by other architects. In addition, at least six different schools, a major hospital complex, multiple commercial buildings, and eight religious structures were designed in that mid-century modern style popularized by my dad.

A foundation started by our mother and now supported by her children opens my boyhood home to the public. There are daily public tours in addition to experiential and hands-on educational programming for students of all ages, beginning at the fourth grade level. Almost 20,000 people experience our home and my dad's studio each year.

I left for the US Army in 1956, returning two years later to finish college, meet my wife of fifty-nine years, and raise two children. Still today my sisters and our children all love and support a continued interest in that mid-century modern architecture.

Growing up in that amazing architectural masterpiece, which we now call the "Home and Studio," had a profound effect on my life. I believe that my dad's positive approach to his profession and to our upbringing has given me a similar outlook. Whatever I do, it must be honest, have humility, and be enthusiastic.

I distinctly recall him saying more than once about an idea, "I don't think that has ever been done before," which was likely correct, and it meant that we should try it. In my late teens, we raced nineteen-foot sailboats, and I was always reading every sailing book I could get my hands on. We were total beginners. I remember cutting up and resewing a brand new spinnaker sail because Dad was convinced we ought to try a new flap idea for the sail. It did not work very well. But we tried.

Dad patented a way to take the leftover potash from burning coal and make building blocks that interlocked together. They were substantial, rhomboid-shaped blocks with a hollow core for insulation. A wall built of these blocks may feature one side as the finished interior surface and the opposite side as the complete exterior wall. The finished interior and exterior surfaces have the look of one-foot square blocks. The blocks worked well for many of the homes he designed, including our own home. This time his idea worked very well.

Many years later, I was in the flying business. A company I owned with a partner was a dealer for small aircraft. We sold the

One of Mike's endeavors was building a factory
to build new Classic Waco F-5s.

airplanes, repaired them, taught folks how to fly, and flew charter passengers all over the Midwest. One day my partner suggested that we should actually build an airplane. Wow, that seemed like a far-out idea, as well as a big stretch for our little company.

But with a positive outlook, an honest approach, and lots of enthusiasm, we pulled it off. We found that the Federal Aviation Administration seemed willing, so this new idea to resurrect an old prewar biplane was feasible. My partner liked a certain 1935 model, an open-cockpit biplane built by the Waco Aircraft Company that was popular in its day. We created brand-new versions for current pilots who wanted to go back in time and own and fly an open-cockpit biplane. What fun it was.

This positive attitude has certainly been ingrained in my life, and today I often recall, "I do not think that has ever been done before." So let's go try it. And be sure it has HH&E!

four

What Makes Johnny Run?

by John D. (Chimo) Arnold

John David Arnold, author, business executive, and international-ist, was born on May 14, 1933, in Boston. A lifelong lover of music, he played clarinet and formed a jazz band at Harvard. He married Dorothea DeFeyo in 1956, just before entering the US Army. Honorably discharged, he joined Polaroid as assistant training and development director. Several nights a week, he ran seminars for other companies in Massachusetts and Maine, and on Saturdays he taught business communications at Northeastern University. Eventually he joined a Princeton, New Jersey, firm where he co-developed a problem-solving, decision-making seminar, was the first regional manager, and then became director-international.

In 1968 he left the company, moving his wife and three sons back to Boston to start John Arnold ExecuTrak Systems, Inc., an issue resolution, conflict management firm. For the next forty-plus years, John worked with top executives, mainly at Fortune 100 corporations, all over the Americas and Europe, helping them confront the most difficult issues they faced. His work formed the basis of his six published books about executive decision-making and issue resolution, accelerating product development and market entry, conflict management, acquisition integration, and organization revitalization.

Still involved in music, he served on the board of World Music and the Philharmonic Society of Orange County and co-founded the Laguna Beach Music Festival. He married Diane Summers Arnold twenty-five years ago and lives in Laguna Beach, California, when he and Diane aren't traveling around the world.

"**W**hat possesses you to work as hard as you do, even when others see little likelihood of you achieving what you'd hoped?"

That was the question my executive assistant asked me many years ago at about 3:00 a.m. as the two of us were finishing up a feedback report for the integration of UK-based Parker Pen and France-based Waterman Pen into Gillette. Working at that hour was nothing new to us; I prided myself on the decision analysis/ conflict management/issue resolution process I had developed and copyrighted. It was helping many organizations including Ford, Pillsbury, Abitibi-Price, Canadian National Railways, Honeywell, St Paul Companies, and the city of Spokane address some of the thorniest issues they faced and resolve them. But it required an enormous number of hours, tremendous energy, and extreme focus to achieve the impressive results that I demanded of myself and which my clients expected from me.

Back then I answered: "I don't know. I just plain don't. Wish

I did, 'cause then maybe I could do something about it and not tear around the world as I do."

Now, so many years later, I do know the answer, having reached way back in my memory bank during these last happy years with my wife, Diane, far from my intensive, innovative, dynamic corporate projects. You may look askance at some of what I reveal about myself, but with me, what you see is what you get. No pretense, no facade.

—

We lived at 484 Lowell Avenue in Newtonville, Massachusetts, in a dark duplex. My father was a sweet and intelligent man, but stern. He didn't smile often and seemed to come home from his work very tired. The closest my father ever came to expressing affection for me was when he occasionally called me "Sunny Jim." The only time he really laughed and seemed to relax was on weekends when we would go to visit his brother Bim or his sister Ethel.

My mother was troubled. As a child, I would sit on the stairs watching her crying while she haltingly played piano—lovely music, beautiful "Claire de Lune" and "Pavane for a Dead Princess" and lots of Chopin. Why was she so sad? It scared me.

I still remember my first day of kindergarten. My mother took me there, and when she was about to leave, I began crying and grabbed hold of her dress, refusing to let go. The teacher finally helped my mother wrestle my hands away. Through tears, and feeling an overwhelming sense of dread, I watched my mother leave. Every day for some time this was repeated, until I finally attended without a fuss, succumbing to authority—something I've resisted doing since then on significant occasions.

I remember being sent away to live with an uncle and aunt in Gardner, Massachusetts, for a month when I was eight or nine years old. They were very stern, and I spent every day alone in their house or in the field yearning to go back to my home and not understanding what had happened to my mother. This became somewhat of a cycle; several times I would be sent to live with relatives for a week or more because my mother was "going away." Later I learned that she was going to mental institutions and receiving shock treatment for depression.

One of my early memories as a child was the flood of Eastern European immigrants coming to our small home to stay for a night or two before moving on to promised work in the fields of Pennsylvania or Ohio. They were fleeing Catholic priest-driven and fascist pogroms and coming to this country to escape the beatings, being forced out of their homes, or burned alive because they were "the Christ killers." Like many other Jewish women, my mother sometimes would welcome these starving men, women, and kids as they got off the boat from Europe or the train from New York and bring them home. Although I didn't understand what they were saying in languages foreign to me, there was no doubt about the fear and anguish I saw on their beaten, emaciated faces. I can still, with anxiety, picture them today.

We lived next door to the Bilezekian family. Nancy was my age, and we sometimes played together. She or her mother would bring over Armenian food, hummus, baklava, and what we called "cigars and cigarettes" (stuffed grape leaves), from whence my love of Middle Eastern food has lasted to this day. In fact, when Diane does not make oatmeal with blueberries and strawberries for breakfast, I eat lavash with lots of hummus.

It was from the Bilezekians that I learned about the horrible Turkish genocide of the Armenians. It was incomprehensible to me how the Turks could do this to their neighbors—starve and force them to walk hundreds of miles under a terribly hot sun or in freezing cold and then murder them just because they had a different religion or were of a different race.

Our upstairs neighbors, the Merowiczes, added to my anxiety. They had terrible arguments, yelling and screaming at one another. I never could understand why, because their son, Marvin, seemed like a nice person. Why did they fight? So much about life was unsettling, stomach-churning, frightening.

While many of my childhood memories involve fear, I also remember what great comfort I found in music. As a young child, I happily sat on the floor in the late afternoon in dim light listening to *The Singing Lady* on the radio telling stories about little Ivan, Prince Igor, and other wondrous tales. Her voice, the stories, and especially the background classical music made such a great impact on me. When I got older and listened on the radio to *The Lone Ranger* with Tonto, *The Green Hornet* with Cato, *Bulldog Drummond*, and *The Shadow*, I became so fascinated with the background music that I started going to record stores to try to identify the composers: Tchaikovsky and Rossini and Wagner and Reinhold Gliere and César Cui and Stravinsky. Through perseverance (a trait which many who know me say is my middle name), I ended up identifying, believe it or not, sixteen classical compositions used on *The Green Hornet* and twenty-six on *The Lone Ranger*.

Thus was born my lifelong love of classical music. In later years, after my parents were too infirm to continue with their Boston Symphony Orchestra subscription, I took it over and then enjoyed thirty-six years of outstanding performances. I also joined the board of directors of World Music. For the last sixteen years, Diane and I have been season subscribers not only to the marvelous LA Philharmonic but also to the Philharmonic Society of Orange County, on whose board I sat for six years as vice president for programming, bringing in world-class orchestras including the Berlin and Vienna Philharmonic and the Royal Concertgebouw Orchestra. With a partner, I started the annual Laguna Beach Music Festival, now in its nineteenth year.

I am grateful to my parents for having introduced me to music at such an early age by listening to the radio and records. My mother had me take piano lessons, but I hated practicing, so they bought me a small drum set and I started on that. The Merowiczes upstairs complained so much that I finally switched to clarinet. I played clarinet in band and orchestra through twelfth grade but hated having to play solos. When recital time approached, I became so terrified that I worried about it for days and nights until the day came and I staggered through it, so relieved when I was finished. The same was true when I had a part in plays; I always tried to get the part requiring the least speaking.

That anxiety has continued through adulthood whenever I've had to make a speech; although, strangely, when I lead top executive conferences for major corporations here and abroad, I am completely comfortable. Go figure!

And I was shy around girls, especially around Elizabeth White, whom I liked. One day during fifth or sixth grade, my friends and I were at Elizabeth's home and somebody said, "Let's play spin the bottle." When it was explained to me that if the bottle stopped and it pointed toward me, I would have to kiss one of the girls, I became very anxious and wanted to get out of there. It wasn't very long before the bottle indeed pointed towards me and the other end pointed toward Elizabeth. I bolted for the door and raced down her front steps and all the way home.

I was curious about girls, however. One late winter afternoon walking home, I stopped in front of a house in which another girl lived, crossed the front lawn, stole up to the window, and on tiptoe peeked in, hoping to see her unobserved. Somebody suddenly came up behind me and grabbed me, saying "What the hell do you think you're doing?" I was shocked and scared stiff, afraid he would take me to the police. He didn't, but he marched me home and spoke with my mother. When my father got home, he ordered me to lower my pants and gave me a sound spanking with his belt. That put an end to my peeping Tom days.

Down and across the street from our duplex on Lowell Avenue was a cliff and forest. Fun was climbing up there with my friends and playing capture the flag. One day, Elizabeth White joined us. I was hiding behind a tree near the edge of the cliff when I heard her shriek as she emerged from the trees, slipping and falling toward the precipice. With one hand, I grasped a tree branch and reached out with the other and was able to grab her just before she tumbled over the face of the cliff. I was quite the hero, and my deed was written up in the Newton newspaper. (But I never did get to kiss her.)

Although we were a conservative Jewish family, all my friends were Christian. In the afternoons after grammar school, I especially loved to play with Bill Warren, David Harbor, and Alan Rawlings. We loved spinning tops, bucking up 1, 2, 3 to see how many fingers your opponent would put out, shooting marbles and baseball cards against the wall, flipping coins to see who would win, and, as we grew older, playing baseball.

But my family's religious practices came between me and having fun. On Fridays my father would come home from work in the late afternoon, and we would say prayers while he and my mother lit candles. Then we'd have to go to temple and again on both Saturday and Sunday mornings while my friends played baseball. My parents also forced me to go to Hebrew school on Monday, Wednesday, and Friday afternoons while my friends were playing together. It certainly took lots of time away from having fun, and I really resented my father making me do this week after week, month after month. I hated sitting in the synagogue and listening to the chanting of the men in their black yarmulkes and white prayer shawls while they swayed back and forth murmuring their Hebrew language. It felt so archaic.

Many Sunday afternoons we would visit Uncle Bim and his family. He would play records—Tchaikovsky, Rachmaninoff—and would listen to the news from Europe. I remember hearing a broadcast of the Nazis marching into Warsaw and seeing pictures of the horrible Stukas as they released their bombs on innocent people. I lived in fear that the Nazis would sweep into America, so imagine my reaction on December 7, 1941. From that time forward, I hated "Japs," especially as we learned more and more about their inhumane crushing of populations in the Far East, let alone what we later learned about their atrocities and concentration camps.

Watching newsreels of Chamberlain handing over Czecho-slovakia to the Nazis, the welcome the Germans got as they marched into Austria, and their horrific blitzkrieg of Poland made a fearful impression on me. To this very day, I sometimes have dreams about the Nazis. Certainly after the Japanese bombed Pearl Harbor and during the early years of WWII, I feared that the highly disciplined, messianic Nazis with their martial songs would take over this country and slaughter my family and all the Jews. My mother and father talked about anti-Semitism and the Catholic Church accusing us of having been Christ killers. My parents said, "You have two strikes in life because you're a Jew. Don't ever forget it! It doesn't matter how good you are; you just have to fight for everything."

I had an Uncle Mulke whom I loved very much. In his early teens, he had fled Smolensk, Russia, when the czar was impressing Jews into the army and sending them to the front lines as cannon fodder. Mulke was a small, powerful man, a supervisor in a shaving brush company, and a member of the Workingmen's Circle, standing for the rights of free men everywhere. We used to visit him some Sunday afternoons and at their summer camp. Many of the guys at his factory were Irish, and they hated Jews. One day, a burly Irishman called him "you dirty Kike," and Mulke threw him through a window. The Irish never bothered him again.

It was difficult for me to comprehend all this, but I knew I didn't want any part of it, and I grew up quite fearful. I told my parents that as soon as I was bar-mitzvah'd, that was it for me: no more temple, no more Judaism, no more religion. Finally the day came. Unfortunately, I was quite sick, but I carried through and think I did a good job on the pulpit and made my parents proud. As soon as we got home and the party for me began with my friends all downstairs enjoying it, I was sent upstairs to bed so that I wouldn't contaminate anyone. So much for entering manhood!

During the war, our religion certainly wasn't helping Jews, nor was the Bilezekian's religion helping Armenians, let alone the non-Aryan Christian populations in Europe or China. To this day, I continue to feel that so much more horror has been perpetrated in the world down through the centuries by religion than any good it has done. I am very pro-Israel, but it's probably been more than thirty years since I have been in a synagogue.

My father had a good job; he was the only Jew at a Protestant shoe findings manufacturer in Boston. He had changed his name, from Israel Isaac Aronovitch to Israel I. Arnold, and received several promotions. But at some point he found that he could rise no higher because of his religion. So he asked the two owners to buy back the stock he had continued to invest so that he could afford to start a new career. They refused. He left, bitter and virtually penniless.

Eventually he set my mother and grandmother up in our living room with two stitching machines, and they began making raincoats; that is until the Japanese invaded China, Malaysia, and Thailand, cutting off the rubber supply. To survive he came up with the idea of making and selling slipper socks, which he was able to build into a good business.

We moved to Newton Center when I started junior high school, and it was both there and at a different temple where I developed friendships with a group of Jewish boys, several of which I retain to this day. There were also many Irish Catholic thugs, and a "wolfpack" of them often tried to beat up Jewish kids as we walked home from school. I lived some distance from my friends, but when I heard the yell of, "There goes a Christ killer!" I ran like a bat out of hell and never got caught or beaten up.

In both junior high and high school I was an excellent student and read voraciously every story that Jules Verne and H.P.

Lovecraft ever wrote. I guess they were my escape from feeling lonely, from the scary news from Europe about the war, and from my fear about the Nazis sweeping into and across America and slaughtering the Jews. I remember one book during this anxious period that really stood out in my mind by Stephen W. Meader. It's the story of a Jewish boy in Eastern Europe living in the forest who has to flee into a small, German-occupied town. There are soldiers everywhere as he tries to emerge from the woods, so he finally screws up his courage and goes straight up to one man who listens to him and explains how to get away safely. There was one phrase that has stuck with me: "Go straight to the heart of danger, for there you will find safety."

The summer when I was twelve years old, I went with my junior high school friends on a bus to Philmont Boy Scout Ranch in Raton, New Mexico. For one month we hiked, camped out, rode horses all over, and really learned how to fend for ourselves. I loved it; it was a challenging but wonderful experience. The Philmont Ranch and the Wild West movies I loved made such a favorable impression on me that I promised myself I would someday get back out there.

That one month in New Mexico marked the end of my childhood. From that point on, each summer and on Saturdays, I would rise at 6:00 a.m. and walk with my father the mile to the 7:00 a.m. train to Boston to work in his hot, smelly, noisy factory producing shoe findings and slipper socks. I would spend all day in the shipping department and then clean around the sewing, stitching, and cutting machines as well as the men's and ladies' rooms (the latter were worse). We would not arrive home until 7:30 p.m. By high school I had become an excellent packer and shipper, as I am to this day.

Just after I finished ninth grade, we moved from Newton Center back to Lowell Avenue. Number 526 was a duplex, and my Aunt Bess and Uncle Bob moved into the other side. In contrast to my parents, Bess and Bob were both merry in nature; Uncle

Bob loved to tell me imaginative stories about "the Afghanistan twins," which I so enjoyed. Professor Abe lived next door and was often visited by George Schulz. If I'd only realized at the time what a great statesman Schulz would become, I would have tried to get to know him.

Across the street lived Buddy, who was both a good friend and my challenger throughout high school for the best grades. We also competed in the debating club and on the school newspaper. Buddy was suave and handsome, had a beautiful smile, and was very popular with girls. He could talk his way out of a paper bag. But he couldn't beat me in spelling bees, try as hard as he did!

In addition to excelling in the classroom, I was president of the writing club and several other school organizations, played clarinet in the orchestra, and marched in the band at football games. When graduation came, all my friends expected that Buddy was going to be awarded the prestigious Harvard Prize Book, which was given by faculty vote to the outstanding member of the class. I thought so, too. Imagine my surprise and how astonished my friends were when it was announced that I had won it!

I met a girl from Lynn, Massachusetts, one weekend when my mother and I were there visiting a cousin. Some days that summer, I would sweep up as quickly as possible in order to take an earlier train home and then drive to Lynn to see her for a couple of hours, despite being dog-tired. I would then drive back home, arriving about 1:30 a.m., only to rise at 6:00 a.m., have a quick breakfast, and walk the distance to the train station with my father to go back to work. She was my first girlfriend.

She was Christian. All my time living in Newton right through college, I never met any Jewish girls except one whom I liked. They all seemed to be Jewish American princesses. There was one girl, Naomi Danovitch, who really took a shine to me. My friends kept pestering me to date her, but I refused. Looking back, I was a damn fool not to have dated her. I might have learned something about women, but that had to wait until my senior year of college. Even worse, senior year in high school, I became enamored of Merle Mandell. I dated her sixteen times, taking her to the Totem Pole Ballroom in Norumbega, but despite dancing with her all evening, when I said goodbye to her on her doorstep, I never dared kiss her.

In the spring of senior year, I went on a school exchange trip to Clark Summit, Pennsylvania, and sat on the bus next to Mary Vaccaro, who was jolly delightful, but Catholic. We became secret sweethearts as my parents hated the idea of my having a Catholic girlfriend. I would have to wait until they went to bed at night and then run the two miles to her home near my Uncle Bim's, throw pebbles at her upstairs bedroom window, and urge her to come down, which invariably she did. We would sit or lie on the grass together and hug; she didn't want to have to confess to her priest of having done anything worse.

Eventually I pledged myself to her as she did to me. When she went away to Trinity College in Washington, DC, and I went to college at Harvard, I was bereft—so lonely and unhappy. Through those four, long, tortuous years, I stayed faithful to her, until graduation week. Over many years, I've occasionally searched to find what happened to Mary Vacarro but have never been able to discover anything about her.

I applied to just two colleges, Harvard and Williams. I visited Williams first and was very impressed with it, liking the beauty of the area and the small size of the school, in addition to its fine reputation. I've never cared for big cities—Cambridge certainly didn't appeal to me—but obviously Harvard was a marvelous institution. When the Harvard dean of admissions interviewed me, he finally said, "Well, Mr. Arnold, are you considering any other colleges?" When I responded, "Yes sir; just one, Williams," he stated, "Yes, that's a fine school," and added, "Have you made up your mind?" I said, "No sir," at which point he looked at his watch and said, "Mr. Arnold, you have exactly sixty seconds to make up your mind!" My heart was in my throat but at the end of maybe fifty seconds, I blurted, "Sir, Harvard!" and he congratulated me: "Good choice, son; you're accepted!"

While I felt proud, I had some post-decision regret, because I had been very attracted to Williams. I felt that the dean should not have put so much pressure on me to make a decision right away. But on balance, going to Harvard felt good. I was pleased also when I learned that Harvard had refused Buddy's application.

I was assigned to Elliot House, and that was a big disappointment for me due to its elitist, "WASPish" reputation. So I made an appointment to see Dr. Finley, the housemaster, a man of impeccable and formidable reputation. When I entered his office, he said, "Am I to understand, Mr. Arnold, that you do not wish to come to Elliot house?" and looked at me both quizzically and deprecatingly. I responded, "Yes sir; that's correct. I just feel I wouldn't be comfortable here." There was a long pause. As I recall, he didn't seek any further information from me other than stating, "Mr. Arnold, never in the long history of Elliot House has anyone ever refused to come here. Our bar is very high, and you had the good fortune to be selected to join us. Do you really wish to refuse?"

"I'm afraid so, sir," I answered.

"Well, you're a foolish young man. Good luck to you."

It took a deep dive into my psyche to realize what a mistake I believe I made. Happy as I am and proud of my business achievements and the person I am today, my whole life could have been so much easier had I stayed at Elliot House. Yes, I would have had to adapt to the ways of the wealthy preppies, but I could have, and it certainly would have broadened me. I would have met interesting classmates and developed friendships with some who might have eased my entry into the business world. I certainly would have met many interesting women. But I was too shy, lacked self-confidence, and my vision was too narrow, despite all I had read, experienced, and achieved—and I was hopelessly in love with Mary Vaccaro and not interested in meeting any other girls.

So I joined Kirkland House and started out majoring in anthropology. Even though I was fascinated by it, I felt I couldn't earn much money when I graduated, so I switched to psychology. But then I learned that psychology required taking biology and chemistry. I really didn't want to cut up animals or cadavers, so I changed again to English and then to sociology and finally graduated cum laude in social relations.

Harvard was a grind, not only because of my classes and studies, but because I began working five jobs, for the most part simultaneously, during those four years. I started the Harvard Magazine Subscription Agency, going door to door selling subscriptions; I built a Cutco cutlery salesforce of eighteen men and women selling to brides and getting an override commission on their sales; and I was the Bates Shoe Company representative on campus selling shoes door to door. In addition to selling slipper socks from my father's company to Jordan's, Filene's Basement, Interwoven Stocking Co., and others, when the factory was very busy, I would go there to ship merchandise. I also formed a seven-piece jazz band (I was the poorest musician), playing some local gigs at neighboring colleges.

Because I pined away for Mary, I only occasionally allowed friends to fix me up with a date and so I had no social life or did anything relaxing except listen to jazz and enjoy the companionship of my best friend Edgar Clark, with whom to this day I communicate. Edgar was jovial, down-to-earth, very imaginative, and lots of fun, always laughing with a twinkle in his eye. His brother, Peter, was more elitist but very bright and quick-witted. They both appeared to have had a much happier upbringing than I and traveled in wealthier circles with prep school boys. They often had girls around them, especially a Radcliffe friend whom I found most attractive but with whom I never dared speak.

I was president of the Harvard Film Society. As often as I was able to pry time away from my jobs, I would go with one or both of the Clarks to see a foreign film. We even tried to film a short mystery I wrote using an MBTA car in which the murderer chose his victims by following the trail of water from his umbrella to whomever it touched. The trouble was we couldn't quite get the water to pool at the base of the umbrella and trail to the intended victim!

Only in later years did I learn about Edgar and Peter's experience in France during the war. After the Nazis invaded Paris, they fled with their mother (their father having escaped to England) to their farmhouse outside Paris, only for the Germans to make it a headquarters. So they fled through the Pyrenees to England where they were schooled and then came together to Harvard.

As I was in ROTC, during the summer between my sophomore and junior year I had to go to Fort Sill, Oklahoma, for basic training in field artillery and as a forward observer close to enemy lines. I told my father I was not going to sell Cutco cutlery nor work for him but wanted to go back out West and experience the country and the people on my way to Fort Sill. Although the most hitchhiking I'd ever done was one time eight miles from Watertown to Newton, I took $80 and set out on a cross-country journey with a high school friend. On the second day, after being stranded for some hours, he called it quits and headed back home. I continued on.

The first experience I recall from that time was standing at the beginning of a bridge over the Potomac River to Virginia when a car pulled over and a woman called, "Get in."

"Where are you headed?" I asked. "Chattanooga," she said. "That's where I'm headed," I responded and then said, "You know, you really shouldn't be picking up a man you don't know." She burst out laughing and asked, "Are you dangerous?"

"No!"

"Okay, if you want a lift, get in." So I did.

When it got dark, I took over the driving, and we climbed up the mountain of Shenandoah. It was 1:00 a.m. when we came over the top and started down the other side; I gently put my foot on the brake but nothing happened. I did it again and again and again. I yelled, "Nedra, wake up!" As we started hurtling down the mountain, she sat up. "What's happening?"

"There are no brakes; I can't stop the car!"

We were gaining speed on a winding, twisting road, and it was very dark. I pumped the brakes frantically. She reached over between us and yanked up on the parking brake, but that didn't do any good. The car was hurtling down the road, and I shrieked, "Nedra, I can't stop it! I've got to crash the car, sideswipe it."

"You can't; it's my boyfriend's car!"

The headlights showed another S curve and nothing beyond. As we went into it, I swerved hard so that the car went over on just two wheels; we were partially in the air in our seats. But, thank God, as we rounded the curve, there was a slight incline ahead instead of another downhill slope. The car slowed and then started rolling back. My foot kept pumping, pumping, but no brakes. I pulled the car way over off the road, getting as close to the trees as I could, and it finally came to a halt as my foot kept pumping up and down. I couldn't slow my heart, it was beating so wildly. I whispered to Nedra, "Don't say a word; just don't breathe."

We sat there in silence for probably fifteen minutes, hoping against hope that the car wouldn't move, and when it didn't, I slowly opened the door and got out very carefully, gingerly closing it. I said, "Nedra, I'm going to find some rocks, put them behind the rear and front wheels, and lie down behind the car so that if it starts rolling back, I can stop it."

And that's just what I did—crazy as it seems today. I guess that I was naïve in so many ways. In this instance, I thought that by lying behind the car, I could hear it if it started to move, stand up, and stop it from rolling over the cliff! The handsome knight coming to the aid of the distressed princess. The foolhardiness of that plan was only brought home to me some time later.

No cars passed us either way the rest of the night. At about

4:30 a.m., I slowly rose from the road, went around to the window, and told Nedra I was going to run down the mountain to find a house or a town where I could get someone to tow the car. I ran and ran but no car ever approached either way until, around 6:00 a.m., a truck approached from behind carrying Nedra in the passenger seat. The driver stopped and yelled, "Jump in the back!" so I scrambled in and held onto the boards as he plummeted down. What we discovered was that the '49 Studebaker had gone into overdrive when we crested the mountain and drove down the other side. "Overdrive" was something I'd never heard of, nor had Nedra. Eventually we arrived in Chattanooga. When we got to her house, she invited me in. I wanted to but was afraid and told her that I really had to continue on to Fort Sill. So back up went my thumb to continue my journey.

My time at Fort Sill couldn't pass soon enough, and I was so happy when I hit the road again. I had some other interesting experiences hitchhiking before I eventually got home, and even more crazy adventures when I hitchhiked across the country after my junior and senior years. Those two summers I hitchhiked 13,500 miles through forty-three states, working my way around by lettuce and cherry harvesting, being a short order chef, and doing other odd jobs.

On one adventure, I had gotten all the way to California but had been stranded all day by the side of a lonely road. It was getting dark, and I was thirsty and hungry. I found a phone and made the obligatory Saturday call to my folks—not letting on that anything was amiss—and I was bone weary when a car jerked to a stop and a big guy leaned out the window and ordered me to get in. It didn't feel right, but I asked, "Where are you headed?"

"Portland, and we want you to drive us there," the driver said. He climbed in the back seat, and I climbed in and started driving. His companion in the front seat took out two bottles and said, "My friend, you do the driving, we'll do the drinking, and we'll all get along just fine!"

Hours passed, and I was so tired, trying to keep my eyes open and worrying about my passengers as they laughed and cursed. My military B4 bag that held all my meager belongings was next to the door by my left foot. They started talking about the cat house they were going to visit and told me I was going with them.

"What's a cat house?" I asked, and they bellowed with laughter.

"You mean you never heard of a cat house?"

"No, not really." They started hooting and hollering. The guy in the backseat started punching my back and they giggled.

"That's where you get women, and you're gonna have a really good time!"

"Well, thank you, but honestly I'm not interested. I'm in love with a Catholic girl back in Boston, and I really don't want to meet any women." That really pissed them off. The guy in the backseat pulled out a knife and stuck the blade behind my neck and said, "You're gonna come with us, that's it!"

I was terrified. Bone-tired with two angry drunks and eyes that stung like crazy, I did the only thing I could do. "Okay," I said. And as we pulled into the outskirts of Portland, I jammed on the brakes for a red light, grabbed my B4 bag as I wrenched the door open, and ran for my life. Thank God they didn't have a gun, because they would sure as shootin' have shot me right then and there.

I learned more during these hitchhiking experiences about human nature and how to get along and communicate with people than from all my classes at Harvard. Back at college, I wrote up some of my hitchhiking stories and sent the article to the prestigious *Saturday Evening Post*. One day I received a two-page, single-spaced, typewritten letter whose gist was: "Mr. Arnold, this is fascinating, and you write very well. The experiences you describe show your bedrock American honesty. We wish we could publish it, but our readership are mothers and fathers, and they would take a dim view of their children reading this and wanting to hit the road as you did."

Harvard was no fun whatsoever. I deeply regret the extraordinary time I invested in earning money and the waste of what could have been four exciting, inspirational years. But "Sunny Jim" had been raised to slave away and achieve; I never heard my parents utter the word "love" until they were in their fifties, after a tragic family event. What was worshipped was achievement. And that I accomplished!

Perhaps six weeks before graduation, I asked permission from my friend Marshall to take on a date someone he was "two-timing," meaning dating her while he was also dating—and much more fond of—another woman. On a double date with Marshall, Dottie seemed like fun. We had some more dates and eventually got pretty serious.

After graduation I hitchhiked down south and then across to Fort Bliss, Texas, again having some interesting—and a couple of dangerous—experiences. I hated the Army regimen for anti-aircraft officers and was really lonely, missing Dottie terribly. On weekends I was often the only guy left in the barracks while the others went into Juarez to find women or just have a good time. But I stayed on base and drank quarts of grape juice to dull my pain.

We were all on tenterhooks because we feared being sent to Korea given what was happening there with North Koreans and Chinese overrunning our anti-aircraft units. One day I went to the base commander and asked him why we didn't get instruction in bayonet training so that we could better defend ourselves in similar circumstances. After listening to me, he said, "That's a fine idea, lieutenant!" and within a couple of days, we were all undergoing bayonet training. Somehow the word got around that some lieutenant had proposed it; everybody wanted to know who was that son of a bitch? Well, nobody ever found out.

We got our orders. Most of my class went to Korea, a few were sent to Greenland, and I was fortunate enough to go to Germany. As soon as I found out, I called Dottie and told her, "I'm going to Germany, and I think in all fairness to you we either should get married, or we should not have anything further to do with one another. So think about it." The next day I got a telegram: "Flying down to marry you!", which she did. Roger Masters, my Harvard classmate who had just arrived for his training, and the justice of the peace, were the only other people at our wedding. No one from either of our families came.

We honeymooned in Acapulco, Mexico. The very first day lying on the beach, I was so badly sunburned that the hotel had to wrap me in tin foil. I laid in bed for several days, an inauspicious start to our life together. Only several days after returning to Boston, I flew Dottie over commercially to Germany before me. Fortunately a family friend who was with the Voice of America met her at the airport and made her comfortable. I arrived two days later, and we traveled to Mannheim, where I reported for duty.

The battalion commander was distressed to find that Lieutenant Arnold was a married man with his wife in tow. There was no space at the *Kacerne* (barracks) for us, so I had to find an apartment and did so in Viernheim nach Mannheim, a little village with no other Americans. We lived on the first floor in a tiny flat. Every day when not on maneuvers, I would walk at 6:00 a.m. to the streetcar and travel to the barracks. At first I was very apprehensive about not only living in a foreign village but about walking by a forest and wondering if any Germans would spring out and try to kill me. Eventually I began to look at living in Germany as a new adventure.

But I really hated the Army. Our battalion exceeded Army limits for the percentage of blacks versus whites; we had over 70 percent. The officers were all white, and all (except one from New Jersey) came from the Deep South: Georgia, Alabama, Louisiana, and Mississippi. Not only did they dislike northerners; they hated "niggahs." Whether in the *Kacerne* or on bivouac (we were in the field three months out of the year), most days we would have coffee at 10:00 a.m., and my battery commander, burly Captain Dunda (behind his back, the other northern officer and I referred to him as "Dundahead") would say, "I have a [bleeping] niggah coming up tomorrow for court-martial. What should we give him, boys?" Loud and clear, everybody would raise their coffee mugs and yell, "Give the niggah bastard a six by six!" (This meant six months detention in prison and two thirds of his pay deducted for that period of time.) It never mattered what, if any offense, the soldier had committed; they were out to screw him.

God, I was so appalled by this, in anguish over such rotten injustice. And as the new second (and later first) lieutenant, it was my duty to be defense counsel for these unfortunate guys. Try as hard as I could, in my nineteen months with the battalion I didn't win a single case. Even when twice I brought in the judge advocate general, they couldn't win against these officers committed to railroading the black soldiers.

One day I pulled my motor pool guys together (not all were black, so I was taking a hell of a chance), and I said, "Look, the dice are loaded against you. You just can't win against these Southern bigots. I'm out for revenge! I want to form 'Arnold's Marauders' and attack them when we're on bivouac. Are you with me? If you choose to join me, you must pledge never to reveal who we are or name any member of our team." Well, every last one of them agreed, even the whites, because they thought it was despicable of the officers to be so unjust.

And so, whether at Grafonvehr near the East European border, where we were supposedly defending West Germany against hordes of East German and Russian tanks potentially invading through the Fulda Gap, or up at Todendorf near Kiel on the Baltic Sea, we did some night attacks against different units of the battalion with dummy ammunition and tear gas grenades. One night I had the distinct pleasure of lobbing a tear gas grenade into the tent of our battalion commander, Colonel Mathis, a bigoted Southerner.

There was then quite a search to try to determine who was responsible. No one betrayed us. To play it safe we laid low, until one night at 1:00 a.m. my battery commander and our first sergeant came into our battery perimeter in a ¾-ton truck from living it up in a local *Gasthaus*, and we hit them from both sides! Captain Dunda came staggering out screaming, "I know it's you, lieutenant! You goddam Kike! I'll have your ass, you Jew-boy piece of [bleep]!" I hightailed it to my tent and had just gotten into my sleeping bag when he rushed in, picked me up, and hurled me against the side of the tent. "You're screwed, you son of a bitch! I'm bringing you up for court-martial." Which he did.

I was terrified, because the court-martial board consisted of officers in the battalion, many of whom believed I was guilty. All it would've taken was one soldier to name me. But none did. I really had guts, because at one point I remember saying to the board, "I would rather have Private First Class Choquette (who was black) by my side in battle than any one of you!" Try as hard as they did, putting lots of pressure on the guys in my motor pool, they could not find me guilty. But ever after they hated me; I was damn lucky they didn't skin me alive.

When I finally got my orders to come back to the States, we were up again at Todendorf on the Baltic. The weather was colder, more dreary, and more rainy each day. We failed to hit more than one or two radio-controlled aerial targets, and I was at my wit's end. I was so sick at heart, so hated my situation, so lonely for Dottie. I lost it. Early one morning I went AWOL and hitchhiked 550 miles back to Mannheim.

I remember walking into our apartment on a Tuesday morning. Dottie took one look at me: "What, what are you doing here? You're not due back for another week!"

"I know. I flipped out. I just couldn't take it anymore."

"Oh my God, you're dead! They're going to court-martial you. You're going to spend your life in prison!"

"I know. That's probably what they're going to do."

Well, somebody up in heaven must have liked me. The Army didn't court-martial me; instead, they shipped me home earlier. Sometime later I received in the mail a commendation with an honorable discharge from the same Colonel Mathis whom I had teargassed.

With my earnings from Cutco Cutlery and my other jobs at Harvard, I bought a home in Framingham, worked for my father for a couple of years, and then responded to a Polaroid ad: "Does the fact that few people use their full talent in their everyday lives bother you?" I joined this exciting, fast-growing company as number two in training and development. I also started, with a friend, Managerial Development Associates, creating and conducting management development seminars for small companies and for the New England Shoe and Leather Association. Polaroid simultaneously paid me as a full-time employee and as a consultant in communications.

Three nights a week during the winter, I would leave Polaroid, drive up to Portland, Maine, and conduct seminars, arrive home well after midnight, and resume work at Polaroid first thing in the morning. With another friend, in November each year we used his van for our mobile-home toy service, selling toys door to door. And if this wasn't enough, on Saturday mornings during the college year, I taught business communications at Northeastern University. The fear and anxiety that had settled deeply into my psyche during my childhood and driven me to excel as a student caused me to attack my career with the same zeal.

Though it was exhausting, I loved the work, especially at Polaroid, where I thought I was doing so much good. But one day the head of human resources told me that some people were uncomfortable with me. This really floored me. I tried so hard to figure it out and finally came up with the answer: When I had negative news to convey, I was so uncomfortable that I smiled. And the recipients read into my smile that I was enjoying being the bearer of bad tidings! I said I would work to overcome this, but it was suggested, unfairly, I thought, that I find employment elsewhere.

So I did, with Kepner-Tregoe and Associates, Inc., a Princeton, New Jersey, problem-solving/decision-making seminar firm. My decision-making and communications work and articles had come to their attention, and they hired me as their sixth employee. Ben and Chuck asked me to move to Princeton, so I immediately put my home up for sale. That very first weekend, I got an offer $300 below my asking price. It seems incredible, but at the time with my growing family of two small boys, the considerable pay cut I had taken to join the firm, and my side businesses, I refused to accept it. Only nine months later did the house finally sell for a much lower price, and by then the firm had grown to over a dozen smart, achieving employees. Had I moved when requested, I would have been on the inside of the tiny cadre; by the time I moved there and was running around the country developing and conducting conferences, I was just one of the senior staff. Vital opportunity missed!

My first day on the job I flew from Boston to Minneapolis to meet my boss, John Zimmerman. Zim was a harsh taskmaster. I no sooner got off the plane than he drove me to his home and put me to work helping him develop a program for middle managers. He and I would work until 3:00 a.m. each morning, sack out, and rise at 6:00 a.m. to continue developing the seminar and materials. We had a deadline. Some weekends he would let me fly back to Boston on Thursday night, working on the flight, and return to Minneapolis on Sunday evening, showing him what I had accomplished and immediately resuming work with him.

I liked Ben, Chuck, and Zim and was dedicated to the task. Zim and I met the deadline, launched the program, and I was soon running five-and-a-half-day intensive conferences (and sometimes the executive program) for major corporations around the country. I also developed a train-the-trainer program for major corporations and ran that until Ben asked me to move to Chicago as the first regional manager.

Dottie was pregnant with our third child, and we made the move in December. I ran the region until I took over overseas operations and was soon spending a week in Europe, returning Friday night to Chicago, and often leaving Sunday for South or Central America. So consumed with the need to succeed, I had little time left for family life. Derek, Keith, and Craig were growing up largely without a father, and I was unhappy in my marriage.

The associate who replaced me as central regional manager operating from Detroit told Ben that I was falsifying sales reports to make myself look better. That was simply not true. But, coupled with the discovery that I was having an affair with an employee in Princeton and the rejection by Ben and Chuck of my proposal of concepts I felt would improve our product, I decided to leave and start my own firm, John Arnold ExecuTrak Systems, Inc.

We moved from Chicago back to Wayland, Massachusetts, and for one long year during which I came close to going broke, another fellow and I continued developing my proprietary issue resolution, conflict management process. Back I went on a cycle of marketing and implementing major organizational revitalization and acquisition integration projects with major corporations in North and South America and Europe. For more than forty years, I helped executive management teams learn and apply the process to analyze and resolve the toughest gut issues facing their organizations, which became fodder for my six published books:

Make Up Your Mind, published by Amacom (American Management Association)

How to Make the Right Decisions, Mott Media

Shooting the Executive Rapids: The First Crucial Year of a New Assignment, McGraw-Hill

Trading Up—A Career Guide: How to Get Ahead Without Getting Out, Doubleday

The Complete Problem Solver: A Total System for Competitive Decision Making, John Wiley

When the Sparks Fly: Resolving Conflicts in Your Organization, McGraw-Hill

My two oldest sons, Derek and Keith, worked in my company, which was a sheer pleasure. Both boys went on to become top executives with healthcare companies, the experience they gained at ExecuTrak Systems having considerably helped them.

After thirty-six years of legal marriage, Dottie and I divorced, and I met my wonderful Diane, who was president of a Boston advertising agency. Diane would take vacation time and assist me on some of my projects both here and abroad. One such project was with the largest non-governmental employer in Peru, the Southern Peru Copper Corporation. This was during the time of the Shining Path guerrilla group, and everywhere we traveled we were accompanied by guards.

I knew a broker who sold companies, and I hired him to find a buyer for ExecuTrak Systems so Diane and I could eventually throttle back. It took three years to convince Diane to move to Laguna Beach after exploring and evaluating venues against our decision selection criteria. We've never been happier than here on Paradise Cove overlooking the Pacific.

So what have I learned from life? What would I like to pass on to my four (soon to be five) grandkids and to younger generations?

First, figure out what you really stand for. What's your inner truth? Then do your utmost to live up to it while doing your best to ensure that your words and actions don't hurt others. I've tried to do this in my own life with lots of minor and some major failures. Second, if your gut doesn't feel right, don't say or do it. Third, face reality. Climate change is upon us. You may never bring home the brass ring, but do your damnedest to make this a better, more humane world. Fourth, don't drive yourself as I have throughout my life. I was raised to achieve above all else, and my anxious nature took that goal to the extreme. But I've learned that it's not the amount of money you earn or the number of accolades you receive that really counts. As a wiser man than I once said, "Life should not be measured by the number of breaths we take but by the moments that take our breath away!" Breathe deeply and live!

Finally, pay it forward. Unless you're destitute, recognize that there are people out there—even right down the street—who are worse off in one way or another than you. Help them in whatever way you can. (This year, I contributed to 104 charitable organizations. Some received only $15 or $20, others considerably more.) If you cannot contribute funding to anyone, at least contribute your time. Help make humanism a greater reality on our spaceship Earth.

five

A Life in the Clouds:
Low and Slow and
High and Fast

by **Gary Cunningham**

Captain Gary Cunningham of Delta Airlines retired in 2001 after almost thirty-two years. He served for six years in the US Marine Corps after graduation in February 1964 from the University of Idaho and commissioning as a second lieutenant. He graduated from the USMC Basic Infantry School Class of H Co 4-64 and earned his Navy Wings of Gold in January 1966. Gary served thirteen months (1967) in Vietnam as a Sikorsky UH-34 helicopter pilot and two

years as an instructor pilot in the T-28 with the Naval Air Training Command. He was accepted by Delta Airlines as a pilot in January 1970 and retired in 2001. While flying Delta's big jets, he served two terms as the captain representative and chairman of DFW Council 47 and two terms as captain representative and chairman of PDX Council 124 of the Airline Pilot Association.

Three of my uncles served in WWII. One fought with the Army in Italy, one fought with the Navy in the Pacific, and one as a fighter pilot over Europe. The fighter pilot did not come home. He was my mother's baby brother. When I left for Vietnam as a Marine helicopter pilot, I can only imagine her concern. My younger brother dropped out of college and enlisted in the Marine Corps in 1967. He did not serve in Vietnam due to his sensitive military occupational specialty code. I have two sons currently serving—one as an Army Ranger and one as an Air Force fighter pilot. Both have served in combat. I have three cousins who served during the Vietnam conflict. I know how concerned their mothers would have been.

My good friend, Ed Nef, invited me to join a trip to Vietnam some years ago. I was reminded of the over 800 combat missions I had flown as well as the sacrifice of the men and women who fought. Ed chronicled that trip with an excellent documentary movie, *The Reconciliation of Vietnam*. He has also produced a very good movie about the ultimate sacrifice of a young American fighting in WWI. It is important that we all be reminded that "freedom is not free." We can never repay the debt to those who have suffered that ultimate sacrifice. Nor can we return strong, healthy bodies to those suffering from the ravages of combat. When I wear my Vietnam ball cap, my heart is always warmed by the child or adult who says, "thank you for your service."

For all the mothers, fathers, brothers, sisters, aunts, uncles, cousins, and concerned Americans who have watched our young men and women put on a uniform representing their commitment to make what may be the ultimate sacrifice, let's all say, "THANK YOU FOR YOUR SERVICE." Memorial Day provides an opportunity to remember and pay tribute to the sacrifices made by so many great Americans. God bless America!

—

Born in 1941 in Santa Monica, California, I spent my early years growing up in Venice and enjoying the beach, but I did not learn to juggle chainsaws. We moved to a new subdivision carved out of the orange groves in Whittier, California. I played football and basketball at Whittier High School and earned an NROTC scholarship to attend the University of Idaho, where I sought easy access to the skiing. Unfortunately, the skiing occupied more of my time than my academic pursuits, so my four-year program became four and a half, and I graduated in February 1964 with a commission as a second lieutenant in the US Marine Corps.

All regular Marine Corps officers were scheduled to attend the Marine Corps Basic Officer Infantry School at Quantico, Virginia. My class, H 4-64, graduated in December 1964. The Secretary of the Navy, Paul Nitze, was our graduation speaker. He was very candid about the Gulf of Tonkin Resolution, which was used to elevate US involvement in Vietnam. In early 1965, many of my classmates landed on the beach at Danang.

Even though I had never considered pilot training, some of my buddies thought it would be a good idea, and I agreed. I must confess the inducement of flight pay amounting to a 50 percent increase over the $222 monthly pay of a second lieutenant was a factor. I traveled to NAS Pensacola, Florida, to my next level of USMC training as a naval aviator. My Basic School roommate and good friend who influenced my decision changed his mind once we entered the flying phase and elected to go to artillery school. There was some competition for grades to qualify for advancement into the jet pipeline. I made the cut, but in spite of some friendly pressure, I decided to be a helicopter pilot.

After earning my Navy wings, I traveled to USMC Air Station New River, North Carolina, in January 1966 to join my squadron, HMM 261. Not long after my arrival, the squadron boarded the USS *Okinawa* for a cruise to the Caribbean. I received some additional valuable training, and, after returning to New River, I received my qualification as helicopter aircraft commander. In December 1966, I was headed for Vietnam. I joined my next squadron, HMM 361, in Okinawa that same December when they were preparing to return to Vietnam just in time for Christmas and a quick dip into the East China Sea.

We were doing training with some Marine ground units and had lifted off from a practice field when, just after "feet wet" over the water, our helicopter lost power and we began an auto rotation into the water. This maneuver was one we were well trained for, and it was successfully executed. I was the pilot in the left seat, and as the rotor blades came in contact with the water the aircraft rolled over on its side, and I quickly became submerged. As I sank deeper, I exited through my side window and pulled my Mae West deployment cord. It operated as advertised, and I quickly came to the surface, but a Marine passenger who had been trapped inside the belly and decided to pop his Mae West prematurely (while inside the helicopter) welcomed me as a life buoy and attempted to re-submerge me. I managed to calm him into submission, and the Mae West kept us both afloat until we were linked to safety by our squadron mate.

—

Right after liftoff in September 1967, I looked back to see the base at Dong Ha, just south of the DMZ, exploding as an attack by the Viet Cong rained down rockets that hit the ammo dump and the fuel storage area. I was busy with the medivac mission that morning and was unable to return for fuel, so I refueled from the USS *Iwo Jima* just offshore. I returned to Dong Ha after dark to find the squadron had retreated to Danang and our base was deserted. I landed my H-34 to retrieve at least my toothbrush but had second thoughts as I made a quick run through our squadron area. I knew the Marine regiment we supported was still there, but it was nowhere in sight. My decision to recover the toothbrush was in the below-average category, but I did have plenty of time to review it as I flew back to Danang to rejoin the squadron.

———

Roger Herman, one of my squadron mates from Vietnam, was asked to say a few words at a funeral for Doc Eagles, a corpsman who flew with us on our medivac missions. He asked me to fill in, as Doc Eagles and I had flown together on a mission we would not forget. I met Doc Eagles the morning he showed up as the corpsman assigned to our medivac mission. He was well-armed with bandoleers of ammo and a grease gun, ready for whatever. My copilot was the commander of the H-46 squadron, which was grounded for mechanical reasons.

We received a call from a Marine recon team in trouble up near the Hivan Pass, north of Danang. We arrived over a thick canopy of trees and observed the yellow smoke that the recon Marines provided to mark their location. I told my copilot to monitor the radio so I could talk to my crew chief on the integrated communications system. We were receiving some small arms fire, and I told the crew chief to let the Doc know what the circumstances were. I didn't think it was a good idea to lower him down through the thick canopy. The crew chief told me Doc Eagles wanted to go down and provide the care the Marines desperately needed. He got on the hoist, and while we hovered over the canopy of trees, unable to see the ground or the corpsman as he got off the hoist, the crew chief said he was clear, and we departed.

I turned my radio back on to listen to the Marines on the ground. The first transmission was, "Where is the corpsman?" I knew Doc was in trouble because of me. We were almost out of gas, so I refueled at Danang, then I flew back to where we dropped Doc Eagles. The recon team still needed help and was getting some air support but no corpsman.

Two days later, the Doc got back to Marble Mountain, where our squadron was based. His story was one of heroic valor and survival. While he might have demonstrated righteous anger over my actions and judgment, there was none of that. When he got off the hoist and saw only bad guys in black pajamas and no Marines, he knew he was in a fight for his life. He battled his way down the mountainside to Highway 1 and managed to get on a bus back to Danang.

Doc Eagles spent three tours in Vietnam. It has been said that that you will find no atheists on the battlefield. I think it is hard to find an atheist at a funeral. It is important for us to find peace from the scriptures in times of sorrow. In Revelation 21:4, it says: "He will wipe every tear from their eyes. There will be no more death or mourning or crying or pain for the old order of things has passed away." We celebrated the life of a true American hero; may he rest in everlasting peace.

—

My tour of duty in Vietnam ended in December 1967, and I left my squadron at Subic Bay in the Philippines, where we had arrived from Vietnam on the USS *Okinawa*. The ship then carried my squadron back to Vietnam, arriving just in time for the Tet Offensive. I began my trip home on circuitous travel orders,

THE UNITED STATES OF AMERICA
THIS IS TO CERTIFY THAT
THE PRESIDENT OF THE UNITED STATES OF AMERICA
HAS AWARDED THE

AIR MEDAL
(GOLD STAR IN LIEU OF THE SECOND AWARD)
TO
CAPTAIN GARY W. CUNNINGHAM, UNITED STATES MARINE CORPS
FOR
HEROIC ACHIEVEMENT ON 9 OCTOBER 1967

GIVEN THIS 7TH DAY OF OCT 19 68

Gary's Air Medal certificate.

westbound with stops in Bangkok, New Delhi, Tehran, France, Germany, and New York before traveling to NAS Pensacola, Florida, to report in at the Marine Air Training Detachment, Col. Conroy USMC ("The Great Santini") commanding.

I did make a brief stop in Stuttgart, Germany, to take possession of my new Blaut Rouge 1968 Porsche 911. I felt the car would enhance my image and new assignment as a captain in the USMC and as a Naval Air Training Command instructor pilot. The following two years were very eventful. I purchased a small beach cottage on Pensacola Beach. I married my wonderful wife, Dana, with whom, by divine intervention, I had managed to reconnect after our graduation from the University of Idaho with the class of 1963. I was assigned to NAS Whiting Field and was an instructor pilot with almost 1,500 hours in the T-28 Trojan trainer aircraft. I was awarded an Air Medal for Meritorious Service for 820 combat sorties from February to October 1967, in addition to two single-mission Air Medals previously awarded. At the end of my two-year assignment, I reluctantly decided to leave the Marine Corps and accept a pilot position with Delta Airlines.

———

The second phase of my flying career began on January 5, 1970, with my new hire class at Delta Airlines. After completion of training as a second officer on the DC-8, I was assigned to Dallas Love Field pilot base. I still remember how impressed I was one dark, rainy night as we approached landing with a strong crosswind at New Orleans with a rather small captain at the controls of a rather large Stretch DC-8 and me at the engineer panel. After a successful landing and as we taxied in, I realized what a challenge I had accepted in my new career with Delta. After a brief period flying out of Love Field, the pilot base was moved to the new DFW Regional Airport, where I spent the next twenty-nine years prior to my upgrade to the MD-11 and flying out of the Portland International Airport.

As my wife and I moved to our new location in the Dallas/Fort Worth area and began our search for a new home, we discovered six acres available in Argyle, which is north of the DFW Airport. We moved a mobile home onto the vacant six acres, and I began to build our home. As a reserve pilot, I did have a lot of time to work on the new house. We spent some exciting nights being buffeted by strong winds in our mobile home, trying to decide whether or not to head for the ditch along our gravel road. After an afternoon visit with the postmaster of our small town and discussing our adventures in the wind, we agreed it would be a good idea to anchor the mobile home. My life experiences so far

UNITED STATES MARINE CORPS
HEADQUARTERS FLEET MARINE FORCE PACIFIC
FPO, SAN FRANCISCO 96610

The President of the United States takes pleasure in pre-
senting a silver star in lieu of the forty-first AIR MEDAL
to

CAPTAIN GARY W. CUNNINGHAM

UNITED STATES MARINE CORPS

for service as set forth in the following

CITATION:

"For heroic achievement in aerial flight while serving as a Pilot with Marine Medium Helicopter Squadron 361, Ninth
Marine Amphibious Brigade in connection with operations against
the enemy in the Republic of Vietnam. In the early evening
hours of 3 September 1967, Captain CUNNINGHAM was Section Leader of a flight of two UH-34 helicopters enroute to Dong Ha when
he received an emergency medical evacuation request to extract
a seriously wounded member of a Marine reconnaissance team six
miles southwest of Con Thien. Upon his arrival over the designated area, two A-4 Skyhawk aircraft were conducting air strikes
against the North Vietnamese soldiers who had advanced to within
100 meters of the reconnaissance team. Realizing the serious-
ness of the situation, Captain CUNNINGHAM contacted the fixed-
wing aircraft pilots and requested that subsequent attack runs
be made parallel to the approach run of his helicopter in order
to expedite the mission and provide uninterrupted support during the medical evacuation. Upon landing, he observed that the
Marines were twenty meters away. Disregarding the enemy fire
and demonstrating exemplary airmanship, he lifted his aircraft
into a hover position, air taxied across the zone and landed
near the casualty. Then, when the Marine was aboard, he executed a low level, high speed takeoff through the hostile fire,
receiving a hit to his aircraft, and safely departed the area.
Captain CUNNINGHAM's courage, exceptional aeronautical ability
and unwavering devotion to duty at great personal risk contributed significantly to the accomplishment of the hazardous mission and were in keeping with the highest traditions of the
Marine Corps and of the United States Naval Service."

FOR THE PRESIDENT,

V. H. KRULAK
LIEUTENANT GENERAL, U. S. MARINE CORPS
COMMANDING GENERAL, FLEET MARINE FORCE, PACIFIC

Silver Star letter.

had not prepared me for the challenges of living in a mobile home on the Cross Timbers slope of north central Texas.

My wife accepted a position at Lewisville High School teaching French and Spanish. The location was a forty-five-minute drive, and she carpooled with an early settler who was a longtime resident and lived on the family farm just west of our six acres. She learned a lot about the history of our rural neighborhood. John's Well, an early gathering spot of this area where the local settlers would park their wagons, enjoy a camp meeting, and visit with their friends, is just a short walk south of our property.

We started our family in the house I had built, where we were relatively safer than in the mobile home. As our family multiplied, so did my building efforts to expand the size of our home. In the beginning there were two of us. When we reached five, we decided the time was ripe to move out of the construction site. We split the six acres into two acres and the house that I had built, and we began to build on the remaining four.

The Rural Argyle School District was a wonderful find, and our three children grew up with friends whose parents all knew each other. There were no secrets, and we all paid attention to our children's education and social and athletic activities. Argyle did not have a high school, so our children attended Denton's high schools just to the north. Our two sons and one daughter were good students and active in many extracurricular activities. We went to church on Sundays, and our faith in God and the redeeming grace of Jesus was an essential part of our spiritual life.

Our oldest son received an appointment to the US Air Force Academy and graduated with the class of 1994. Our second son received an appointment to the US Military Academy at West Point and graduated with the class of 1995. Our daughter was accepted at the University of Colorado and graduated with the class of 1997. All have received advanced degrees, one PhD, one MD, and numerous masters. They had a wonderful mother and a Marine father.

My wife continued teaching French and Spanish during the time our children were in high school. After our three children were in college, she accepted a position with a major textbook publisher as a national language consultant. I became more active in the Airline Pilot Association as an elected representative.

———

My Delta Airlines retirement flight was scheduled for September 18, 2001, destination Tel Aviv, Israel. Two weeks before that flight, Dana joined me in New York before my scheduled trip to Narita, Japan, and we went down to the World Trade Center theater ticket outlet for show tickets. We saw a show, and she joined me on the flight and layover in Narita. My retirement flight was cancelled because of 9/11 and substituted with a one-way NYC-ATL flight on September 20. I received the traditional firehouse greeting (a water salute spraying over my airplane from fire trucks on either side) after landing and taxiing in at Atlanta. The rule then was pilots could not be in the air flying after their sixtieth birthday. My birthday was September 21.

Our family has been truly blessed to live in a great country where freedom, duty, and honor to God are important measures of our greatness. A family unit full of love and respect for God, country, and those who serve to protect our safety and our freedoms is the essential ingredient to our survival as a nation.

six

Cold War and Remembrance

by **Douglas Hartley**

Doug Hartley served in various capacities as a Foreign Service Officer with the US State Department for more than fifty years. He served in Denmark, Austria, Italy, Greece, Yugoslavia, England, Brazil, and Haiti. He was an observer for the Organization for Security and Cooperation in Europe in Kosovo, Croatia, Bosnia, and Serbia in the aftermath of the Balkan Wars of the 1990s. He now lives in Falmouth, Maine, and frequently visits his children, grandchildren, and great-grandchildren in Brazil and England.

The first and most important thing for most of us is our own wellbeing and that of our families. This can never be taken for granted and ultimately affects us more than anything else. I have been extremely fortunate that the various wars I've lived through, with one exception, haven't directly affected me. The exception was leaving England shortly after WWII as a boy of five for Baltimore, Maryland. My mother kept things together and brought up my older sister and me through the war years until my father was demobilized after serving in the British Army. He wrote me touching letters during those wartime years. One of the most thrilling moments of my life was in 1945, when I was ten, to see my dad after more than five years of his absence. He enjoyed the camaraderie of Army life, but his war experiences left him in a profound depression that led to an early death in 1949 at age forty-six.

I wonder why it is that God has given me the gift of life so that at age eighty-five I have lasted beyond anybody in our family's recorded history except for an aunt on my mother's side. I've also been blessed with healthy offspring who now include two greats, one girl and one boy, who join a cluster of ten grandchildren.

Another blessing: I've never been financially strapped. Owing to my great-grandfather, who amassed a fortune in the wool business at the turn of the century, and the generosity of friends and relations, our family has been reasonably free from worry in comparison with many others.

I've also been fortunate during my life to spend more than fifty years with the State Department, thirty of which were spent overseas at various consulates and embassies. I never was sent to any "hardship" posts with security or health hazards (with the possible exception of Belgrade in the early sixties). Thus we were able to give our children a good education and safety as they grew into adults. Some posts were challenging professionally, but others were less so. Nevertheless I wanted to assure my family that I put their interests first, ahead of my own career.

My life changed in January 1946 when my father and I returned to England, land of my birth, for boarding school in St. Leonards, Sussex, a war-torn, gloomy place on the English Channel. He had spent years in the British Army and was determined to "toughen me up" by exposing me to a British prep school. From there, I spent another four years at Eton. Immediate post-war England was in shambles. Marshall Plan funds were funneled into the continent. England was saddled with huge wartime debts, a tired population, and a socialist government that nationalized most industries and imposed a bewildering array of permits to do almost anything. I recall that my cousin Dickie Dickinson had to wait months for a permit to tear down his garden shed. The result of all this was that England lagged badly; food remained rationed for years. I remember being surprised, while I was at school, to receive shipments of eggs from Denmark at a time when the ration in England was one egg a week.

I attended Harvard as an undergraduate, after which I joined the US State Department as a very young and wet-behind-the-ears Foreign Service Officer. I suppose it was natural that I should gravitate toward employment with lots of overseas content. I had always enjoyed travel. I took a solo trip around Europe and the Iron Curtain when I was eighteen and a voyage from Rome to Paris on a Lambretta motor scooter at age twenty-one. A short stay in the Russian zone of Vienna piqued my curiosity about Russia and the rivalry between the two countries. I saw their anti-US propaganda featuring lurid posters proclaiming our alleged use of germ warfare in Korea. What happened to have destroyed the wartime alliance I remembered, when Soviets were lauded as heroes in the press, in the movies, in my comic books?

At home, McCarthyism had a baleful effect on our country. I was ardently anti-McCarthy, as were almost all my friends and family, but many neighbors encouraged him, owing to their unreasoning fear of "monolithic" communism destroying our way of life. Did we need to help them by inciting fear and distrust

Harvard classmates Doug (right)
and John Arnold, author of Chapter 4.

among our own people? Furthermore, there was no dialogue between the two. Like Trump nowadays, many people secretly supported McCarthy. This type of inflexibility, this Manichaeism, plagues us today.

In March of 1956, I married Deborah Wait from Boston, and we headed for Washington. I had first tried and failed the tough Foreign Service entrance exam as a junior in college, then tried and failed again until, finally, by dint of a cram course I took in DC, I succeeded in passing that and the oral exam. It was a terrifying experience being grilled by three senior retired officers. When I finally entered into service in September 1956, I was twenty-two, for a short time the youngest (and certainly among the least experienced) officers in existence. That was when Imre

Nagy led the Hungarian Revolution with the calamitous arrival of Soviet forces. The US, via Radio Free Europe, had given the impression that we would intervene. I felt at the time that Secretary of State John Foster Dulles was being too hard-nosed and that our foreign policy was intent on fighting the so-called Sino-Soviet Bloc when we should have concentrated on widening the split that was already occurring.

My family and I spent eighteen months in Copenhagen, where I gave out visas and was later rotated to the economic section of the embassy. I was far younger than anyone else but was fortunate to have Hugh Teller as my boss, an old-style Foreign Service Officer who had been around. My assistant was the very talented Jorgen Werner, a local Danish employee who had been heavily involved during World War II in getting Jewish refugees over the Øresund (a body of water between Denmark and Sweden) to Malmö and Helsingborg on the Swedish side. Copenhagen was a low-key post, and there was plenty of time for leisure and parties. When I was suddenly transferred to Salzburg, Austria, I departed after an epic round of parties. We had made many friends, as much because of our youth and capacity for alcohol as anything else.

Salzburg was a center for processing US visas for Hungarian refugees who had escaped the 1956 uprising. Our small unit was located at one of the refugee camps below the Münchberg castle. We lived in a small castle of our own on the hill above the camp. We met and partied with a group of Czechs and Hungarians who had escaped as the Iron Curtain fell over their countries. Our maid was an ethnic German who had fled ahead of Soviet troops on their rampage through Germany to Berlin.

Next was ten months studying Serbo-Croatian, followed by an assignment in Belgrade. Yugoslavia, now divided into six independent nations, was the first place the US government determined that, though Communist, the country was independent from the Soviet Union. The idea of an immutable Sino-Soviet Bloc should have been shattered but was later replaced by the Domino Theory. The latter became an excuse for our disastrous intervention in Vietnam, where so-called liberals like McGeorge Bundy egged on presidents Kennedy and Johnson to a mass intervention, and we all know the consequences of that. My posting in Yugoslavia in 1960 showed me that Yugoslavia was indeed independent and going its own way, which was an uncomfortable mix of state control and, increasingly, free enterprise.

Again and again our intelligence was either faulty or not getting up to the decision makers. We were caught totally by surprise when the Soviets sent Yuri Gagarin to outer space. Gross intelligence failures and cozy relationships between Foreign Service officials and the leadership in power tended to warp our judgment on what was really going on within a society.

A stint in the State Department's Office of East-West Trade showed me the various factions for or against trade liberalization with the so-called Soviet Bloc. I strongly believed that the Bloc was vulnerable and that the various Eastern European countries could, by virtue of trade and cultural connections, be spun away from mother Russia. Later, however, my focus was on Cuba and my task to help enforce a trade blockage after the missile crisis. It was obvious to me that our efforts would have little effect on Cuba's relatively uncomplicated economy. Its wants could be provided by the Soviets, who supported the economy by wholesale imports of Cuba's one key export: sugar.

In Washington there was a clear divide between the hawks and the doves, which played out in various forms and in various theaters. The CIA was a house divided against itself; hawkish elements in the operations branch were often in conflict with the more cautious folks in the intelligence areas. In those days, the Department of Defense was hawkish while the Commerce Department (with whom I worked closely) was pulled this way and that by those who wanted any opening (Polish ham) and those who saw trade as bolstering communist regimes. State tended to be more flexible; we didn't want to make waves.

———

The 1950s and 60s were marked by unrest and turmoil as new blocs were formed from the ruins of the war and colonial powers displaced, while our focus was exclusively the containment of communism, seen as enemy number one. During the Kennedy years, I was amused to see how African leaders always played up the communist threat and thereby ensured huge US aid payments, both civilian and military, much of which no doubt went directly into the pockets of dictators.

Meanwhile we ignored the potency of other forces, such as religion, in capturing people's emotions. It always seemed strange to me how a religious nation such as ours could have been so completely unaware of the potency of faith as evidenced in our disastrous intervention in Iran in 1956 and our backing of a corrupt and incompetent Shah who was loathed by the non-elite of Iranian society.

The 1970s saw our defeat by the Vietnamese, where our intervention came from the mistaken notion that if communism won anywhere, others would follow. We tended to back regimes in Third World countries that were accommodating to our companies working there, such as United Fruit in Guatemala. Embassy contacts would all too frequently be with the guys in charge of the ministries, not with opposition leaders. However, pointed messages from the field citing possible problems with State Department directives were often ignored. The humiliating defeat in Vietnam quenched our thirst for foreign adventures for a decade, until the invasion of Kuwait by Saddam Hussein in 1990.

Russia has always had an ambiguous relationship with the West. It's not unlike the blue versus the red states here and southeast England versus the north and west of that country. After 1990 we had a rare opportunity to establish good relations with the successors of the Soviet Union. Much of my career was during the Cold War, and I saw the strength of our democracy, our culture, and our ideology overcoming the static Soviet system of state control. With the fall of the Berlin Wall, I felt that this was a logical time to embrace Russia in the community of nations.

Following the confused and often drunken Yeltsin, who many Russians thought was a buffoon and a tool of the West, Vladimir Putin became president. In the US he was heavily criticized for brutally putting down the Chechen. This was, however, before we ourselves had to confront Muslim religious fanatics. Despite his and others' misgivings about the US invasion of Iraq, Putin assured President Bush that he wouldn't try to undermine our efforts there. After 2001 he offered aid, which Washington refused. Our bombing of Belgrade on Easter Sunday was deeply unpopular in Russia, a fellow Slavic state. NATO's expansion to Russian borders seems to have been in contravention of previous assurances.

Of course, so much anti-Russian talk and actions these days are political; the Democrats view it as a great way to further damage Trump. If so, Putin was sadly misinformed about Trump's dependability. Perhaps he was also motivated by the frequent snubs and insults about Russia and about him personally from both Barack Obama and Hillary Clinton, and maybe by aggressive marketing in Russia of our ideas by politically-connected NGOs.

The annexation of portions of Ukraine including Crimea were arbitrary acts, but perhaps understandable ones. Crimea is or was the Norfolk, Virginia, of Russia, the site of the Russian fleet. Ukraine is, in Putin's view, in danger of becoming part of NATO. Less forgivable is Putin's blatant interference in our election processes and his threats to destabilize many of the former Eastern European satellites of the USSR.

Trump, to give the devil his due, and for whatever reason, has tried to improve our relations with Russia. He has failed partly because of Putin's own hostility and because of the Democrats' knee-jerk reactions to Putin's Russia. Whatever the justification, Putin is now a sworn enemy, continuing to play his clever game of chess so long as we have no coherent foreign policy and an impulsive President.

———

Deborah and I had four children, Virginia, Alexandra, Charlotte, and Richard, between 1957 and 1964. They accompanied us to our many overseas posts, enduring changes of schools and friends cheerfully and uncomplainingly. Deborah did a great job bringing them up and giving them love and security. This was helped by the string of nice places we were sent—Copenhagen, Salzburg, Belgrade, and Milan. It was good for the family, but not so good for my career. I would have been better off in the trenches at the State Department or in one or two hardship posts. I probably could have had Washington assignments had I chosen to do so, but I preferred to live overseas.

Shortly after a transfer from Athens back to Belgrade in October 1972, I learned that Deborah had been seeing a Canadian Foreign Service Officer with whom we had been friends in an earlier tour of duty in Belgrade (1960–1962). We lived an uncomfortable two years together, and, having told our distraught children, she left for Canada for a new marriage and a new life. With some difficulty, I arranged for a transfer to London. My two older daughters were in school there, and since I had sole custody, it seemed best to bring the two younger ones there so that we could be together as a family unit. While in England, I met Annie Macbain, and our daughter, Sibby, was born in 1976. After four years at our huge embassy on Grosvenor Square, I was given a new posting at Salvador Bahia, Brazil, via language training in Washington. I was due to arrive at my new post in June 1979.

In May 1979, I married Sondra Otey from Memphis, Tennessee, after a whirlwind romance of five months. We met at a mutual friend's house. She had decided to leave Memphis following a divorce. She accompanied me to Brazil and was a lively and beautiful presence who delighted Brazilians and Americans alike. Although she had had no experience living or working overseas, she became a huge asset to me.

After I left the Foreign Service in 1986, I re-upped with the State Department as a retired officer and went to work declassifying documents. I received more challenging assignments than I had in the course of my career, including several stints in postwar Bosnia, Serbia, Croatia, and Kosovo, plus a four-month tour of duty in Haiti. The Foreign Service's in-house training plus a natural aptitude for languages made me perhaps more marketable as a retiree than some others. I ended up with reasonably serviceable French, Italian, Portuguese, and Serbian, plus a smattering of other tongues that have been useful as a tourist, such as German, Danish, Spanish, and Greek.

Sondra and I stayed in our lovely apartment on Wisconsin Avenue, just down the street from the Washington Cathedral. We also built a house in Cushing, Maine, an isolated community on the mid-coast area right on the sea, where we spent the summers.

Following the Baltic Wars, I became an election observer of the Organization for Security and Cooperation in Europe (OSCE) in Bosnia, Kosovo, and Croatia. I worked at our posts in Belgrade (just before Montenegro left) and Naples, Italy, where my Italian language skills were sorely tested by the Meridionale accents of the natives. In the 1990s and early 2000s, I bicycled on several occasions through France with an old and dear friend. In 2013 and again in 2014, Sondra and I rented apartments in Rome and Paris. To escape the long Maine winters and our isolated home, we also vacationed at Turks and Caicos Islands and Anguilla and took two wonderful voyages in full-sailed clipper ships from Barbados through the Antilles.

In 2007, without explanation, I stopped receiving orders to continue my work on declassification. This propelled Sondra and me to sell our apartment and move permanently to Maine, where we made friends and entered into village life.

As to my accomplishments, I feel that I have not done enough for my fellow man. I volunteer at food banks, play the piano at retirement homes, briefly drove an ambulance, and served as president and, for many years, as board member of the Cushing Maine Historical Society. But in comparison with many others, my contributions have been meager at best. In years past I was a guest lecturer on cruise ships along the Amazon River, through the Mediterranean, and on the *Queen Elizabeth 2*.

One day my old Foreign Service colleague and classmate Ed Nef, who had referred to my "European vacation" in comparison with the hardships he reportedly experienced in posts such as Guatemala and Senegal, called me to say that he was making a documentary about Vietnam and wanted me to be the music director. "Why?" I asked. "I've never been to Vietnam and know nothing about their music!"

"Never mind," he replied. "You used to play the whole Grieg Piano Concerto at Harvard." This was a gross exaggeration, because all I did was play the opening bars, which are so simple that any untutored pianist can manage them. So I listened to some Vietnamese records and tried to compose music tonalities that I could only hope would pass muster when and if the film was shown in Vietnam. Thankfully, audiences seemed to approve, as there were no complaints when the film was shown nationwide in Vietnam as part of their "liberation" in 1975.

Through Ed, I produced the music for various documentaries about places such as Senegal, Mongolia, and Vietnam, which I either composed or found appropriate music for. This experience was invaluable and led us to make a documentary about my father's oldest brother, Charles, who was killed as a second lieutenant with the British Coldstream Guards in Cambrai, France, in November 1917. The film was made in the town of Fontaine Notre Dame (Northern France), where after the "war to end all wars," my grandfather erected a monument to Charles's memory. This monument was a focal point for marking, in November

2017, the 100th anniversary of the battle. Many of the townsfolk joined members of our family at the site of the monument to render homage to him and all others who had helped to liberate them in both wars.

———

In July 2012, Sondra found a small tumor on her left breast which was malignant and removed. After intensive radiation treatment, it appeared that she was free of cancer. In April 2015 we attended a cousin's wedding in Arkansas. She seemed to be in great form. She went on to spend a few days with friends in Alabama while I flew back to Cushing. When I drove down to Portland about a week later to meet her, she seemed to be disoriented. Her speech was blurred, and she had trouble writing. After a few days, I took her to the emergency room, where she left by ambulance to the Maine Medical Center in Portland. There doctors successfully removed a malignant brain tumor. She was put on chemotherapy, which seemed to be going well through October, so well that we decided to travel to England for ten days in November. Together we went to the theater and did a lot of walking in the area of Trafalgar Square in London. We attended a moving Remembrance Day Service at the Guard's Chapel by Buckingham Palace, the same church my father had attended while he served with the British Coldstream Guards during the London blitz.

Sondra was very tired, however, and had no appetite. In November we traveled to my daughter's house in a small village in Devonshire, England. We were hoping to see our first great-grandchild, but his mother was late. After a few days there we flew back home. We had friends to our house for Thanksgiving. Then we got bad news from the last chemotherapy session. On December 10, 2015, Sondra was admitted to Mercy Hospital in Portland, where she died a few days later. She was able to see her great-grandson, Indy, via the internet.

I was shattered by her death. Sondra was almost nine years younger than I, and it had never occurred to me that she would go first. Both of us had carved our new lives together and each had learned a great deal from the other. I learned about Southerners and their culture.

Some people, like the Ulstermen, nurse their grievances, while others don't. When I visited Vietnam in 2017, I was greeted not just with courtesy but with genuine interest. After all that their parents had gone through, the younger generation seemed to be really enthusiastic about the US and its people. On the other hand, some American Southerners, especially older ones, still nurse grudges harking all the way back to "the War of Northern Aggression," as some of the more rabid put it. It will take us some time to wipe out the vestiges of the racism of the post-Civil War epoch. The interesting thing is that many African Americans still feel more comfortable in the South, and many Southerners feel more comfortable with blacks than with northern white people. Sondra was a real liberal in the best sense of the word and held no prejudices against anybody. We were both helped by her understanding and respect for the largely mixed-race population of Salvador, Brazil.

After her death, I continued to travel, though I found it less fun being alone. I'm afraid that many people feel uncomfortable with single people, be they female or male, as if they have a certain unpleasant aura about them. But I did spend a month in southeast Asia and two weeks on a cruise up the Danube river from Bucharest to Budapest, visited England several times to keep up with family there, and attended a fine family reunion of twenty-one in Portugal in 2019.

Coming back to our isolated, cold house in Cushing in midwinter was a chore. In May 2018, I put it on the market. Sondra and I would usually flee Cushing for Portland, Maine, during the bad winters. Although Portland has a mere 75,000 people, it feels and acts like a city far larger. It's brimming with fine restaurants

Doug's family in Portugal, 2019.

and a lively theater and concert scene. For us, it was the big city. I found a house in an over-fifty-five development in Falmouth, just a few minutes from downtown Portland.

Once established, I set about finding friends, old and new. I joined two music clubs—one held at St. Luke's Cathedral and the other in private homes. I also found a wonderful piano teacher who teaches at Bowdoin College in nearby Brunswick. Through her I was able to join in recitals and concerts at the Portland Conservatory of Music. I also started work at the Falmouth Food Pantry. Portland has been the site of many refugees, mostly from Africa and the Middle East. I found my language knowledge, especially Portuguese and French, to be a considerable asset. I was even able to use my Serbian for a Bulgarian Russian and Poles who showed up! I've started volunteering to give ESL lessons to our new immigrants. I've become involved in Opera Maine, which has one big production per year, and they are superb. I also started back on tennis last winter.

The atmosphere in Portland is so different from DC. For a start, people aren't so hipped on politics. Though there are of course lots of Trump supporters and shrill liberals, in the main they are pretty moderate.

Looking ahead, I am most disturbed by climate change and glad to see the young so involved. To get people to change wasteful ways, to discourage the use of plastics, to cut down on consumption of just about everything, will be no easy task, especially here in the US. We personally—and the economy itself—breed waste, whether it be instant obsolescence or individual habits. Even recycling is rare in many parts of the country. Food is wasted; our food pantry throws away all unused food it receives. How is it possible to have people going hungry in this country? Paper is wasted. I remember in Serbia following elections we wanted to throw away a ballot box. One of our local workers urged us not to destroy it because it would make a good fort for his children. Waste is built into our society. It will take a revolution to change this unless the younger generation steps up to the plate, which, in these early days of crisis, they seem inclined to do.

In 2018 I received a letter from Bosnia. It was from the son of the Hasanovic family. In 1998, while serving with the OSCE, I spent a month living with them in their war-damaged house in the town of Sapna, close to the zone dividing Serbs from Bosniaks (Muslim Bosnians). The coexistence established in Bosnia following the Dayton Accords is uneasy. While some of those who fled the ethnic cleansing of the Balkan Wars (1992–1995) have returned, the town is economically depressed. Arab money has flowed into Sarajevo, but much of it landed in the pockets of real estate developers and corrupt politicians. Sapna's main employer, a power plant, is still operating, though at

15 percent capacity, and its agriculture of small holdings can't compete with imported products.

The people of Sapna have accepted the dislocations of war but resent the impact of globalization, which they see as a way to redistribute wealth to those who already have it. This isn't just about the former communist world; it's a worldwide phenomenon and destroyer of village life. On a trip to Senegal, I visited villages populated almost solely by women; the men had gone off to seek employment, most likely on rafts across the Mediterranean. Globalization has certainly helped some escapees from village life to reinvent themselves in more urban settings. However, for many democracy doesn't seem to provide an answer. The same doubts about the benefits of democracy are clearly seen in the rise of populism, as witnessed by support for Donald Trump.

So many of us sit in front of our TV screens exclusively watching our favorite channels (Fox News or MSNBC) and venting our frustration. It might be good if from time to time Fox News listeners tuned into MSNBC and vice versa. Many of my liberal friends, when asked if they ever watch Fox News, seem to be proud to say no. If you want to know what the other guy thinks, that's the best way to do it, avoiding the most inflammatory broadcasters on both ends. And if you want to make a difference, there's no point in sitting in front of your TV and wringing your hands. Also worth remembering: while the screen reminds us endlessly of the horrors of war, it rarely portrays the lives of the millions of people who aren't living in fear or in famine.

I suspect that many old fogies like myself are content with our lot. Most of us, and certainly I, have the means to live decently and can afford retirement homes if we need them. Although we've made many mistakes along the way, we've "fought the good fight," and we've come out of it more or less unscathed. We're probably out of danger in this world. Shouldn't we be pretty happy about that?

seven

Dealing with Scarcity and Thrift in Switzerland after World War II

by **Robert Nef**

Robert Nef was born in 1942 in St. Gallen, Switzerland, and has three sisters and one brother. He studied law in Zurich and Vienna and received a master of law degree from the University of Zurich. He worked as a teaching assistant and research fellow for the chair of law at the Swiss Federal Institute of Technology (ETH) in Zurich between 1968 and 1991. From 1979 to 2007, Robert was head of the Liberales Institut in Zurich, a small think tank in the tradition of classical liberalism devoted to individual freedom and the free market. Until 2008, he was chairman of the Institut's publications: "In

Praise of Non-Centralism, Berlin 2004," numerous books, essays, and articles on issues related to classical liberal principles, the history of ideas, Swiss politics, the economy, defense policy, and critical appraisal of the welfare state. Robert served as editor-in-chief of the magazine Reflexion *(the magazine of Liberales Institut) and of the monthly* Schweizer Monatshefte *(a periodical devoted to culture, politics, and economic issues). He is a member of the Mont Pèlerin Society and the International Society for Individual Liberty.*

Robert Nef is married to Annelies Nef-Nyffeler and is the father of two sons and the grandfather of five.

History is made up of little stories. I was born in 1942 during World War II. Neutral Switzerland was spared from this war, but the army was mobilized and had to protect the borders against potential invaders from both sides. Like most fathers, our father was on active duty almost without a break from 1939 to 1945. Since all neighboring countries (Germany, France, Italy, and Austria) were at war, Switzerland was economically isolated, and food and fuel were strictly rationed. There was no famine, but food was scarce for everyone—including richer people—which had a leveling effect. The wealthy rode their bikes alongside everyone else, and there were hardly any cars on the streets. As a pediatrician, our father made his home visits by bicycle and transported his doctor's bag on the luggage rack.

My first memories concern living with scarcity and thrift. This was not only a result of war and crisis. Switzerland was not a rich region until the nineteenth century, and thrift was one of our national virtues. Even in relatively wealthy families, the rule was that one had to eat the plate empty. Any remnants were carefully cleaned with a piece of bread until the plate was clean. In many families, children were forced to eat everything. With us it was like this: you had to try everything, but if you really didn't like something, you could eat bread instead. During the war, dinner was always the same: semolina porridge with some sugar and cinnamon. You could draw a face on the plate with your porridge. In most families, there was some meat in the evening only for the father, and he ate alone after the children, who had to go to bed by 7:00 p.m. at the latest.

My grandmother, Rose Nef-Kern (1867–1954), had lived through World War I, when there was a real shortage of food in the cities of Switzerland. As war loomed again in 1938, she bought a large quantity of sugar, rice, chocolate, crispbread, and Ovaltine as a precautionary measure, which were kept in a box in the storage area. The stocks were so large that it was possible to draw on them even after 1945. I still remember the small dark chocolate dumplings that remained edible after more than five years. Combined with a piece of bread, they were a hearty snack.

The milkman came with a cart pulled by a horse and brought the milk in open cans and poured it into the jugs provided. The additional orders for cheese and butter were on a list and everything was entered in a special booklet and paid monthly. The "milk booklet" was a common practice, as was the booklet with pending payments in the neighborhood shop. If you wanted to laugh at someone, you said: "He went to school with the milk book instead of the exercise book." The baker brought the ordered bread to households every day. He bicycled and had a big basket on his back. The bread was wrapped in thin white paper. As a customer, you could decide whether you wanted the bread light, medium, or dark. The bread paper was not discarded; it was cut into four parts and used as toilet paper. Since this was usually not sufficient, it was supplemented by newspaper.

The rationing of food during the war years was controlled by food stamps. Only one egg per person was allowed per month. But most people knew people who raised chickens, and we children were sent to a woman in the neighborhood to buy eggs on the black market. But we were told that nobody should know this and that this shopping was something mysterious, forbidden. Sugar was also rationed. For breakfast milk, which was usually sweetened, there was half a piece of sugar for each child, and we strictly controlled each other. Butter had to be spread very thin. Bread could not be freshly sold by the baker, because it was believed that old bread was more filling than fresh bread. The first fresh bread after the abolition of rationing, which took place in 1947, was an event. I still remember the unusual crispness.

In cooking, thrift was significant. It was less about saving money than about respecting the reality of a world where much is scarce. The butter packaging was kept because it was still possible to grease the frying pan with the bits of butter stuck to it. The old bread was kept in a tin box, which had the inscription, "Give us this day our daily bread." One could process the dry bread remnants into breadcrumbs with a mortar and pestle, an activity which we children liked very much. The apples were carefully prepared, even wormy ones. "The worms prefer the very best apples," we were told. I was a slow eater and a dreamer, and I was always admonished, "Robert, *mange ta soupe*" ("Robert, eat your soup"). Sometimes my grandmother used to remark, "Robert, *tu rêves*" ("Robert, you dream"). I will never forget that, and I am proud that I have never stopped dreaming of a better, more peaceful world.

During the war, I remember the sound of the sirens when there was an air raid alarm. In the spring of 1945, large American bombers repeatedly strayed into Swiss airspace, occasionally via St. Gallen (the largest city in eastern Switzerland). You were supposed to go to the basement when there was an air raid alarm. Our grandmother, however, allowed us to stay in the garden and watch, since she apparently assessed the risk of accidental bombing as small, and she may have been curious herself. We were able to watch as a big US bomber was attacked by small aircrafts of the Swiss air force. There was some shooting, which looked like small flashes, but the Swiss usually did not hit their target. It is said that the Americans reported by radio, "You shoot too low." The Swiss would then reply, "We know it."

The Americans were admired and appreciated as liberators. My first impression of "real Americans" was a group of soldiers at the train station in Arosa, Switzerland, in 1946. In the group were also black people, and these were the first non-white people I had ever seen in my life.

Thrift became a way of life during the war years and in the following decade. White paper was rare, and all of our children's drawings were on the back of old printed matter. Cardboard boxes were carefully kept, and the paper of Christmas presents was folded nicely and reused, along with cords and ribbons. Old postcards were collected and sorted not only because of the stamps, but also for the pictures; books in those times were rarely illustrated. Before the invention of plastic, yogurt came in waterproof paper cups, which were washed out and stored.

The mail was delivered with unbelievable intensity. The postman came three times a day, and the daily newspaper had three editions, one in the morning, one at noon, and one in the evening. There were three different newspapers in the city: a liberal, a Catholic-conservative, and a socialist. The newspaper delivery was free, but at Christmas the postman expected a tip.

Peddlers came to the front door regularly. They were the poorest people, and we often bought something like soap or shoelaces, even if we didn't need them. Beggars rang the door a little less often. Our grandmother had an iron principle: no cash. "If I give him money, he will go to buy alcohol, and this is bad for his health." So was the reasoning. If he was hungry, he could have a bowl of soup, but this offer was mostly declined. Day laborers who could help in the garden were welcome. They were paid modestly, and occasionally they were given old clothes.

Our clothes were also used very frugally. It was a matter of course that the younger children wore the clothes of the older ones in the family. Since I was the first boy after two girls, this was only practicable with knee socks, sweaters, and sandals. In summer, all children went to school barefoot. Walking barefoot was typical from May until the beginning of the cold weather in October. The soles of the feet were sensitive in the first two weeks, but later one easily jumped on gravel paths.

As a family of a medical doctor, we belonged to the upper middle-class and always had a maid, typically from Austria. The maid lived in the house but had her own washing facilities and was not allowed to use our bathroom. She ate in the kitchen and not at the family table. Emphasis was placed on us as children to not demand anything directly from the maid. The children's relationship with the maid was friendly and without hierarchy. We played together and occasionally sang songs in the kitchen.

We did not have a radio or television in our house during our childhood. Our grandmother had a radio, but she used it only to listen to the domestic comments of her son, the journalist Max Nef, once a week. So we did not listen to music on the radio; instead, we played it ourselves. My grandmother and her daughter Rose often played four hands in the evening. During our frequent visits to our grandmother's house in a nearby neighborhood, we slept on the upper floor and could hear the piano playing after we went to bed. When we went on vacation as a family of seven, one folk song after another was sung in the car. Some of them were older German songs with romantic lyrics; some were soldier songs, silly songs, and even hits. On Sunday morning, we sang with our mother from a songbook with sentimental and sometimes religious children's songs. The songbook was called, *Es singt es Vögeli ab em Baum* (*A Little Bird Sings from the Tree*). She accompanied us on the piano.

My father knew many childhood songs by heart, even in his old age when he forgot many events of everyday life. He occasionally sang to himself while shaving in the morning. With our aunt Rose, we sang French songs composed by the famous music teacher Jaques Dalcroze from Geneva and the folk-style and yodeling Appenzeller songs composed by our great-uncle Albert Nef. At school age, we added the songs learned in school and, since we were all with the Boy Scouts, the rich repertoire of scout songs and so-called "*lumpen* songs" with playful elements.

On New Year's Eve, called St. Sylvester, the whole family met for dinner with a traditional menu: a big sausage, called *balleron*, potato sticks, and beans. After dinner, a *Schnitzelbank* was sung with pictures and verses for all family members, which included particularly funny and typical events from the past year. At midnight, we listened to the bells first and then we sang together the *Landsgemeindelied*, the national anthem of the canton of Appenzell Ausserrhoden: "*Alles Leben strömt aus Dir*" ("All Life Flows Out of You"). The song was sung solemnly, standing. Afterward, we switched over to funny songs mixed with plays and a lot of joking and teasing.

On the day of the ceasefire, May 8, 1945, all the church bells rang before noon. They said it was peace now. I was on the porch swing at home when the peace bells rang, and this rocking was one of my first memories. To this day, I imagine peace as a gentle rocking with bells pealing.

eight

Flashes from
My Early Decades

by **Maja Nef**

*Maja Nef was born in 1938 in Basel, Switzerland, as the oldest of
five children. Her father was a pediatrician. She spent her youth in
St. Gallen and graduated from high school in 1957. After a stay in a
household in England, Maja passed the examination for teachers
in 1958. She taught in a small mountain school and in a home for
disabled children.*

*Maja was especially interested in the children who had greater
difficulties, so she decided to enroll at the University of Zurich, where
she studied psychology and education and graduated in May 1968
with a doctorate. Her first job as an educational counselor/school
psychologist was in Bern at a major cantonal service.*

In 1971 Maja was elected head of a small regional service in Emmental (Canton of Bern). She remained in this position until her retirement in 1999, after which she worked as a freelance psychotherapist for a few years in her small house in the country. In 2014 she moved to a nearby town where she now lives in a senior citizen housing estate.

I was born in Switzerland in 1938. It is important for the understanding of the following episodes to know that I lived in Switzerland, because, especially in the years described below, life in my country was very different from life in the rest of Europe.

In the 1940s we did not have a war in our country, but it raged all around us, and we were not sure if or when it would flood our country. It was not easy, but we were spared. In the fifties we were able to recover from the war in an intact environment. Our industries were not destroyed, our old, medieval towns were unscathed, our archives survived. In the sixties, the pressure of the young generation against outdated, fixed rules, traditions, and constraints was less strong than in other European cities such as Paris or the German university cities, probably because many things were more transparent in Switzerland. The almost direct democracy in our country allowed individual citizens to have a say in many matters. This gave a feeling of security, and one did not feel so much at the mercy of the authorities.

The younger generations fault us for saying that we experienced "the war" (which is always meant as the second World War). "There was no war here," they say. Yes, that is clear today in retrospect, but at that time one did not know. A few early childhood memories show what we experienced then.

In 1940 it was not known whether the Germans would take the route to France via Switzerland. At that time we lived in Kleinbasel, a quarter of the city of Basel, which is north of the

Rhine. It was planned to blow up the Rhine bridges in the event of an attack on the guarded border, so that our part of the city would have been cut off from the rest of Switzerland. Therefore anyone who somehow had the opportunity left to stay with relatives or acquaintances.

I was just over two years old when Mama traveled with me and a rucksack with our most important belongings to St. Gallen in a totally overcrowded train in the midst of the soldiers called to duty. We lived for the next few months in St. Gallen, partly with Mama's parents and partly with my father's mother and sister.

Before 1939 Switzerland used to import a great part of our necessary food from abroad (rice, sugar, coffee, meat, and wheat). Because that was not possible during the war, the Swiss government ordered the planting of all cultivable vegetables, mostly potatoes, in any possible place: sports fields, street borders, private gardens, meadows, and public parks, including all around the cathedral of St. Gallen.

My parents cultivated potatoes and Jerusalem artichokes in our garden. To fertilize the earth, the children had to pick up the horse droppings on the street. There were quite a lot of horses passing by because of the lack of fuel for cars. The boys in the neighborhood ran after the horse manure; as a five- or six-year-old girl, I had not much chance in this fight, but I tried hard.

Until 1948 the important goods for daily living were rationed to distribute them fairly. I remember the coupons for bread, meat, eggs, and chocolate. When we went hiking with the school class, we were offered a snack. We did not have to pay for it, but each child had to bring a coupon. I remember the envelope in which the teacher collected the forty-five little pieces of paper.

Wheat does not grow in many parts of Switzerland, so there was not much bread. For a few years we had a law that bread must be three days old before it could be sold. That way people would eat less bread, because it was not so good. I was about ten years old when the sale of new bread was allowed again. I did not know what it tasted like, because I had never eaten it. I was very excited to go to the bakery with my grandmother and to wait there with a lot of people in a queue until the door opened.

The bread we bought smelled wonderful, and I could hardly wait to taste it. We were walking homewards when my grandmother suddenly stood still and began to tear little pieces out of the bread and eat them. She did not say a word but gave me some of the bread, too. How excellent. I never had eaten a thing like that, and it was simple bread! We continued to eat very small pieces, and when we arrived home, there was very little left of the loaf. That was really not nice. But it was not me who started it!

During the general mobilization in 1939, and then during the entire second World War, all healthy young men served in the military for a large part of the year. Women spent these years mastering the men's tasks. After the war, many women refused to return to the kitchen and childcare, planting the seeds for the women's movement in the years to come.

In my school years, the Girl Scouts—and especially the task of being a leader—had top priority for me. During the war, the scout movement had been forbidden in the rest of Europe and continued to exist only hidden underground. In Switzerland the scouts continued their activities and even helped the Red Cross in the army medical corps.

After the end of the war, the Boy Scouts and Girl Scouts reappeared in the surrounding countries. Traumatized by the experiences with the Hitler Youth, however, the scouts tried, especially in Germany, to remove from their program everything that could have any military or warlike effect.

We had not experienced the horrible impact of the Nazi ideology and were less sensitized. With the Swiss Girl Scouts, we still hoisted and greeted the Swiss flag, attached importance to correct uniform, called the group leaders "*Fuehrer*" (a word that was carefully avoided in Germany), and even marched here and there in columns of four and sang the old songs.

When I look at the songs today that we sang then, I feel quite concerned. But back then, they were important texts for us. A chorus remained in my head from childhood, and I searched for a long time until I found the song that belonged to it. The song's refrain was, "Strong my arm and to you my heart oh my county" and included the lyrics, "forward into a new time/and be it for peace or quarrel." And the Swiss national anthem at that time said, among other things, "Fatherland, you have still sons/never pale from danger/pain us a mockery/joyfully to the quarrel."

After some time, the Swiss federal leadership of the Girl Scouts instructed us to stop singing these "Nazi songs" of the Hitler Youth. They were not Nazi songs, but German songs that were much older and sung long before the second World War. Nevertheless, it was right to erase these witnesses of a dangerous spirit of the age.

In 1957 I finished high school and spent half a year in England and France. I was impressed by the poverty in England and by the still bombed-out capitals, London and Paris. In Germany the reconstruction seemed to be much more advanced, perhaps with help from the US.

In 1958 I took the exam for the diploma as a teacher. I wrote down memories of my first job in a booklet. Since they reflect the typical conditions in Swiss mountain schools, I have translated some of these stories here.

Vermol was where I had my first job as a very young teacher. I lived in the Alpenrose Pension. The school building was farther down the steep slope. The children usually sat down on a shovel and slid down the slope with it. For me there was a little path, but mostly in the morning nobody had walked on it. Snow boots did not exist at that time, nor did pantyhose. Wearing long trousers was not yet suitable for women, either. So I put on thick stockings, knitted by my grandmother, and mountain boots. That went well until it was really freezing cold and the snow reached my knees. On that day, I put on my ski pants.

On that same day, the Catholic priest who was president of the school care came to visit our school. He strongly disapproved of my clothes. He said it was not acceptable for a woman, and especially a teacher, to wear trousers. I complained to him about my problem with the snowy footpath, and he showed compassion. Finally he found a Solomonic solution. He told me to put on an apron over my ski pants. And so I did.

On Saturday afternoons I had two lessons with the first graders. Afterward I wanted to travel to my parents in St. Gallen as quickly as possible, so I would run straight from the school building onto the train to Sargans, which went steeply down through the forest for about an hour. One day I arrived on the train completely exhausted just as it was leaving. I took off my coat and sat down. The people around looked at me strangely and with a smile. What was wrong with me? Oh, I had a linen apron over my ski pants!

One morning an elderly woman approached me on the narrow, steep footpath down to the school building. She asked me if I was the new teacher. She wanted to tell me honestly that she had been very worried at first when she was told that a young lady from the city was coming. The boys in the upper school classes were not exactly kind to my predecessors, and life in this mountain village was rather hard. But when she saw that I was wearing shoes with thick, profiled soles and knitted wool stockings with a plait pattern, she changed her mind. She had also heard positive things about me in the houses.

She was the midwife, she said, and had just come from a woman who had given birth to her twelfth child. It was difficult with so many children, who often found hardly any space in small houses with few rooms. Then a radio message came to our minds, which we had heard the day before. Pro Juventute organized a collection campaign under the title, "Every Swiss child has their own bed." There were still many poor children in Switzerland who had to share a bed with siblings. The two of us, the old and young woman in the snow of the mountain village, had to laugh out loud when we imagined how they would have liked to have twelve beds in the little house of the family mentioned above.

In the Alpenrose, there was a very small television set in the lounge (black and white, of course—color was available much later). At that time, there was only broadcasting in the evening for a few hours, and you could only reach one station. There were very few TV sets, rarely in private households, and certainly not in Vermol. We didn't have a TV at home, and I was not used to watching one. Most of the time it played some kind of vaudeville or cancan show, and the people of Vermol were surprised that I didn't know this world, since I was young and came from the city.

Once, however, I heard the announcement that a broadcast of Duerrenmatt's play, *Der Besuch der alten Dame* (*The Visit of the Old Lady*) was being transmitted from the Zurich *Schauspielhaus* (it was probably the premiere). I wanted to see this, since Duerrenmatt was one of the most famous contemporary Swiss poets. So I sat down in front of the television with a glass of tea.

After a while, two young teachers who were in a ski camp with their class in Vermol came into the lounge and ordered a glass of tea and saw the screen. They began to scold and mock the television. Rubbish, they said, a nonsense, a dulling of the people, and a danger for the children. I sat quietly and continued to watch the famous play with a smile.

There was a pause and the screen displayed the title of the show. The two men became quiet and somewhat embarrassed and watched *The Visit of the Old Lady* with me. It was a life lesson about prejudices, and I do not take myself out. I had only looked because I knew what it was about.

———

From 1960 to 1962, I was a teacher in a home for mentally and physically disabled children. It was a fascinating and satisfying job, as the children were enthusiastic pupils, full of thirst for knowledge. But it was also a strenuous job, because the teachers were not only responsible for the school lessons but for many other everyday needs of the children. The normal working day began at 6:30 a.m. and lasted (with an hour lunch break) until around 9:00 p.m. We had two afternoons a week and three Sundays off per month.

For the school lessons and the care of the children, we had to cope with very simple means. Our working conditions changed noticeably when disability insurance, created by referendum in 1960, was introduced. It took some time before the necessary laws were created and introduced in all cantons, but then every disabled child living in Switzerland was entitled to contributions toward his or her education, and important expenses for the institution could often be covered by this insurance. For example, comfortable wheelchairs or electric typewriters were provided for children who could not use their hands well.

The children did not have very much life experience, and simple activities sometimes became small adventures. One time I noticed in conversation that two paralyzed young girls had never seen a starry sky. So it was a matter of taking two wheelchairs with two young ladies in pajamas out of the house and back in again, unnoticed, during the night. In winter it was too cold, and in summer it became dark late. We chose summer and managed the whole action in the middle of the night. I handled the transport alone, because any confidant could have endangered our success.

Once we went on a trip with all the children. I knew that we would pass by the chapel that was built in memory of the Battle of Stoss in 1405 between the people of Appenzell and the abbot of the monastery of St. Gallen. I used this to teach the children something about Swiss history before the trip. Legend says that the women of Appenzell bravely rushed to help their husbands with hoes, scythes, and poles, and thus achieved a victory. A little schoolgirl remembered this tale, and during a stop at the Stoss Chapel, she asked, "And where are the Appenzell women now?"

—

The sixties were a time of student protests and the "revolution" of the young generation. I studied psychology at the University of Zurich (and Munich) from 1963 to 1968. So I was actually in the middle of the action. I, too, felt the fermenting unrest and turmoil around me, and I took part in one or two protest meetings. The demonstrations in the streets happened outside my window, but the whole thing somehow remained apart from me, or I remained outside the events.

I understood the plight of my generation, but I also understood the older generation. In my childhood, during the war years, I often felt jointly responsible with my mother for my three younger siblings, and I internalized the values of my parents' generation. Our parents had had to give up so much in their youth, during the war, that they wanted to make up for what they had missed in terms of shared experiences, entertainment, culture, dancing, traveling abroad, and amusements. Their main wish after the end of the war was security, prosperity, peace, and order. For them this safety was best guaranteed by strict moral rules, especially in the sexual sphere.

The restrictions, the retreat to safety and peace by our parents' generation, were probably to a large extent what threatened to suffocate the post-war generation. We were looking for progress, openness, freedom, and innovations. We wanted to break out of the stubborn rules and prohibitions; we were fighting against social barriers and discrimination of all kinds.

All this surged around me while I was engrossed by the findings of contemporary psychology, which certainly supported this trend, as I wrote my doctoral thesis. In May 1968, when

Sisters Erica (left) and Maja Nef.

the student unrest in Paris reached its peak, I took my final examinations at the University of Zurich. In June 1968, I began my professional activity as a child and youth psychologist at a cantonal counseling center for educational issues in Bern.

The ideas of the former rebels and fighters for social justice are still present among them, the so-called "68ers." They are said to have social ideals at heart and a state pension in their pocket. Their concerns are close to my heart—I have also fought for women's rights and social justice on a small scale—but somehow I feel caught between two generations. I had been raised with and understood the mindset of my parents' generation. But I embraced the ideals of the younger generation as well. I guess you could say the fight for equal rights for women was more a development than a revolution for me.

nine

My Experiences from 1960 to 1985 in Switzerland

by **Erica Kuster-Nef**
as told to her grandson Nino Rietmann

Erica was born in March 1941 in Basel, Switzerland. In the autumn of the same year, her family moved to St. Gallen. She attended school in St. Gallen until her graduation in 1959. After short stays in private households in Paris and London, as was customary for young women at that time, Erica began her three-year training as an occupational therapist in Zurich. It was the third training course in Switzerland, and she was accepted as member 111 in the still-young professional association.

After a one-year language and study stay with her husband in Paris and Florence, she specialized as an occupational therapist

for the treatment of children with cerebral palsy and worked at
the Children's Hospital Zurich until the birth of her daughter in
1972. Erica was elected to the board of the professional association
and later served as its president. She ran a small private practice
for disabled children.

From 1983 onward, Erica built up the office of the Swiss Oc-
cupational Therapy Association. There it was her task to work for
the development and recognition of the profession of occupational
therapy in Switzerland. She was fascinated by professional and
health politics. Politics challenged her and taught her a lot, and
she has been politically involved, even after retirement, until today.

I was born in Switzerland in 1941. I got married after completing
my professional education. I worked as an occupational therapist
in an outpatient center. It was a particularly impressive experience
for me to treat a young pregnant woman who had lost an arm
in the accidental bombing of Schaffhausen (a city at the Swiss
border to Germany) by the Americans during the WWII. We
thought about how she would be able to hold her baby securely
with a sling around her neck and shoulders and bathe it with one
hand. We practiced with a baby doll.

My husband and I were only allowed to live together after
our marriage, because the ban on cohabitation still existed. Even
holidays together were only allowed after marriage, which played
an important role in our one-year stay abroad in Paris.

The marriage law stated that the man was the head of the
family, provided financial security, chose the place of residence,
and determined the professional activity of the woman. In addition, the woman was allowed to sign hardly any contracts on
her own, not even rental contracts.

After my husband's and my separation (before we were

divorced), our apartment lease was terminated. Therefore, I had to find my own apartment. For my husband, it was no problem to rent an apartment. For me, there were many complications due to the fact that, according to the law, I was not allowed to sign contracts. Many landlords also did not want a mother living alone with her child. Finally, I managed to rent an apartment in my name, as neither the landlady's husband nor my husband had any objections. Financially, I had no significant problems, since I was always employed as an occupational therapist, even if only part-time, and could thus contribute to our finances.

The fight for women's suffrage had already begun at the start of the twentieth century. In Switzerland, according to the constitution, all adult Swiss men were entitled to vote. Men could and had to vote on a constitutional amendment: the introduction of women's suffrage. After they had repeatedly denied women the right to vote, the fact that the majority of voting men voted in favor in 1971 was a great satisfaction for us women.

Before that, women were allowed to found an association and execute contracts in the name of the association. As a board member of a professional association, I was allowed to have a say in the legal regulations of occupational therapy, but I was not allowed to vote on the introduction of the law. We women were part of the Swiss system of direct democracy, but we were not allowed to vote on legislation and proposals or participate in the government elections in the communes, the canton, and the confederation, like the men.

The fight for women's suffrage aroused my interest in politics and my desire to make a difference with my vote. I was particularly committed to equality between men and women, the independence of women from men, and equal pay for work of equal value. Equality was also important to me in the area of pensions, where married women were previously dependent on men. As a divorced woman, I was particularly hard hit by this, because

I did not have my own pension. Due to changes in the law on marriage, divorce, and social security, today divorced women and single women are financially better off than they were.

———

The 1960s in Switzerland were marked by the will and desire of the younger generation to break up the rigid structures of their parents' generation. For me, too, it was clear that the behaviors learned and adopted from my childhood and upbringing had to be revised for my adult life of independence and self-determination.

I joined the Social Democratic Party of Switzerland and took part in rallies. We demonstrated for equal rights, sexual liberation, and for an autonomous youth center that could be used for meetings without constraints. We demonstrated in support of alternative cultures, against police violence and repression, against construction of a new nuclear reactor, and against the Vietnam War.

After 1971, when I had the right to vote, I was also able to support popular initiatives with my signature. In 1972, I voted for the initiative for arms control and arms export ban, and later for the abolition of the army, among many others. Both initiatives were rejected by the people in the vote.

Proposals to revise marriage and divorce law, health insurance, social security and pensions, and environmental and landscape protections were successful—however, often only after the second or third attempt.

Personally, as managing director of the professional association for occupational therapy, I was directly involved in the recognition of occupational therapy as a health profession in hospitals and independent professional practice, as allowed by cantonal health laws and as medical treatment paid for by health insurance. My greatest professional successes were the negotiation of a good collective wage agreement for occupational therapists with the health insurance companies, and the national recognition of occupational therapy training at the university level.

During the Cold War, Switzerland felt threatened by communism and the Soviet Union. Everyone who was "left-wing" or in any contact with the Eastern bloc was suspect and seen as a danger to Switzerland and its neutrality. These included not only the members of the Party of Labor of Switzerland, the successor to the Communist Party banned in Switzerland during World War II, but also exponents of the Social Democratic Party of Switzerland (SP). Therefore, I limited the information about my membership in the SP and my political activities to a close, like-minded circle of acquaintances.

After the suppression of the uprising of the Hungarians against oppression by Russia in 1956, many Hungarians fled to Switzerland and were warmly welcomed here. I was a group leader in the Girl Scouts of St. Gallen when a Hungarian refugee girl, who had been taken in by a family in St. Gallen, attended camp with us. There I got to know a refugee child for the first time and experience what trauma war and flight can leave behind. All the children in the tent helped during the night to hold onto the tent poles and tent entrances in order to counter the girl's fear of possible tanks rolling up from the nearby forest.

My daughter's pediatrician had fled Hungary as a young doctor. He repeated his medical program, his state examination as a doctor, and his residency at the Zurich Children's Hospital in Switzerland in order to be able to run his pediatric practice in Zurich. The psychologist who led the therapy group I attended during my divorce had also fled Hungary at a young age.

In the summer of 1968, I went on holiday with my husband and a friendly couple to Czechoslovakia, where I experienced the so-called Prague Spring, the attempt to create "socialism with a human face." We discussed freedom, democracy, socialism, and the free market economy with many young people on the streets. There was a rousing, euphoric mood of independence. All the more depressing was the news of the invasion of troops from the Warsaw Pact and the violent suppression of the reform movement, which reached us only one week after our return to Switzerland.

These events fueled the fear of a communist revolution in Switzerland. It was only toward the end of the 1980s that the public learned that the state security authorities had set up a file containing thousands of names, some of which contained tens of thousands of entries, about people suspected of carrying out subversive activities. These entries were made accessible on request, and I could not help asking about mine. And there really was a microfiche of mine with the entry that I had contacted a person from the car window who was taking part in a demonstration. I had no memory of such an encounter, and it would certainly not have threatened the security of Switzerland in any way.

I have thought a lot about my experiences as a young, married and divorced woman and mother. I have always been a professionally active person and have been strongly committed to social and professional policies. During this period, within one generation, a lot has changed and developed in Switzerland.

Ten

Taking Stock
1947–1975

by **George S.K. Rider**

George was born in Bay Shore, Long Island, New York, in 1932 and lives in Essex, Connecticut. He attended Bay Shore High School in Long Island, Phillips Academy Andover, and Yale University. He served as an officer in the US Navy aboard the USS Abbot *(DD-629). George worked on Wall Street for forty years starting at Bankers Trust. He worked the balance of his career at Merrill Lynch, Morgan Stanley, and Dillon Read in equity sales and trading, retiring in 1995. He lost his first wife, Betsy Waskowitz, to cancer in 1963. Married to Dorothy Crawford, George is the father of Graham and Jennifer Rider, and the grandfather of Graham Jr., Bradley, Tory, and Duncan. He received the Bay Shore Chamber*

of Commerce Distinguished Citizen Award in 2009; the Andover Distinguished Service Award in 2011; and was inducted into the Andover Athletics Hall of Honor, member of 1948 Undefeated Football Team, in 2019. He became an author at eighty-three with The Rogue's Road to Retirement, *published by Skyhorse in 2015. George has two forthcoming memoirs:* All Ahead Full, Eighty-Eight Years in My Wake *and* Some Call It Paradise: My Family and Fire Island.

*F*inis Origine Pendet: The end depends upon the beginning. Few who knew me in 1947 could imagine that I would begin an essay in Latin and then actually understand what it meant. (I flunked Latin twice at Andover). These words are inscribed on Andover's crest, along with *non sibi*, not for oneself, themes that would define my life.

I was so very fortunate to have had two loving parents who cared for my younger brother, Ken, and me. They taught us, coached us, and instilled in us the importance of religion, love of country, friendship, sharing, and, teaching by example, the benefits of hard work and community service. Dad was a Brit; Mother was the daughter of a prominent doctor, George S. King, born in 1878.

Gramp and the sea were inseparable. He spent his early life growing up on the Great South Bay and had his heart set on Annapolis. He was turned down because of very poor eyesight and reset his course toward medicine. I am the oldest of his four grandsons; three of us became Navy officers, the fourth inherited his poor vision.

Gramp began his practice at twenty-three in Brooklyn, New York. In those days, you did not need a college degree to enter medical school. He went straight to New York Medical School (Flower Hospital) from Patchogue High School, Long Island,

Gramp and his pride and joys.
George is center front.

where he graduated number one in his class in 1895. He graduated number one from medical school four years later.

Gramp began his early practice in Bay Shore, Long Island. In 1917, Dr. King's Private Hospital opened on Maple Avenue in Bay Shore, where he practiced until 1965. He delivered or supervised the delivery of over 5,000 babies during his years of practice. In 1952 he advertised a party at Southward Ho Country Club in Bay Shore to honor those he had helped bring into the world. One thousand arrived, "babies," families, and relatives. The party made the front page of the Sunday *New York Herald Tribune*, complete with a picture of the family.

Gramp also authored two books: *Doctor on a Bicycle*, published in 1958 by Rinehart & Company, and *The Last Slaver*, published in 1933 by G.P. Putnam's Sons. Twentieth Century

Fox later made a movie based on the latter called *The Slave Ship*, produced by Darryl Zanuck in 1937. The screenplay was written by William Faulkner. Starring in the movie were William Baxter, Wallace Berry, Elizabeth Allen, and George Sanders. Mickey Rooney played "Swifty," the cabin boy; it was his first movie.

My favorite story about Gramp was the billing ledger he kept titled "C.T.G." Early in his practice, he inherited many patients who could not pay their bills. He teamed with the new pastor of the Roman Catholic church, Reverend Edward J. Donovan, to treat the poor in the town, "God's poor." New employees in the billing department were often confused when slips came in marked "C.T.G." They were told that the patient was poor, but worthy, and that the entry must be made in the special ledger marked "C.T.G.": "Charge to God." I have his original call book. Some of the entries: Office Visit, 75¢; House Call, $1.00.

Dad worked for Otis Elevator in England. In 1937, he was transferred to the States and headquartered in Yonkers. We settled in Brightwaters, Long Island. When war broke out, he left Otis Elevator to join the British Naval Intelligence. They worked with the Office of Naval Intelligence, headed by William Donovan. Later Dad transferred to the British Ministry of War Transport and participated in the swap of fifty WWI US destroyers for properties in the Caribbean.

The war was never far from our thoughts. During WWI, Dad's converted merchant ship was torpedoed off the coast of Ireland by a German sub that had fueled in Ireland. The sub surfaced and machine-gunned survivors in the water. Dad, only seventeen, was one of a handful to survive. He was creased in the scalp and right knee. His younger brother, Uncle Ken, served with the Commandos and fought with the Gurkhas in India and the Far East in WWII. Dad's cousin Joe Wolfenden was awarded the Distinguished Service Cross for his participation in the sinking of German Submarine 401 in WWII.

The captain of the *Queen Mary*, Ernest Fall, stayed with us during five-day layovers in New York before returning to England with a fresh batch of GIs ready to do battle across the Atlantic. The *Queen Mary* sailed without escort, as she could outrun the German submarines. Fall's hostess gift for Mom was always a rasher of bacon, in short supply here, which the captain picked up on stopovers in Canada.

During WWII, Dad diagramed and showed us on a map the British Navy's engagements and epic encounters, including the sinking of HMS *Hood*, British and German cruiser engagements, the sinking of the battleships *Scharnhorst* and *Gneisenau*, the sinking of the *Bismarck*, the scuttling of the *Graf Spee*, and the sinking of the German super battleship *Tirpitz*. Ken and I reenacted the battles on the living room carpet with our fleet of toy ships. Daily, we hoisted the American flag, two-blocked, with the Union Jack flying from the yardarm. Dad's family in England lived through the dark days, the Blitz, and German tyranny. Nightly prayers always ended with "God bless Grandpa and Grandma Rider, Aunt Eve, Aunt Jess, Aunt Joyce, Uncle Ken, and Cousin Nora."

The highlight of my first fifteen years was spending summers with my brother, Ken, and our parents at Gramp's cottage in Lonelyville on Fire Island in New York. We experienced the great wonders and joys that beach life affords: swimming, fishing, sailing, and eventually summer jobs, bikinis, and beer. The minimum wage back then was forty-five cents an hour. I started as a grocery clerk, deck hand, then dock master, carpenter, garbage collector, cesspool constructor, lifeguard, and bouncer. The jobs paralleled my educational experience at Bay Shore High School, Phillips Academy Andover, and Yale.

A pivotal year was 1947, just two years after the end of WWII, when I left home at fifteen to enter Andover. Ken was a year behind me there. We played hockey and lacrosse together. Our lives at Andover were enriched by classmates from Europe and Asia who had experienced the war firsthand. Knowing them as friends and hearing of their experiences made an indelible impression on me that speaks today as I look at a world that seemingly has failed to learn from history.

The story of Billy Ming Sing Lee, my classmate at Andover, appears in the next chapter of this book. Billy, who grew up in China, arrived at Andover in 1947, the same year I began as a junior (first-year student). We shared four great years at Andover and then four years at Yale, where we were proud members of the Delta Kappa Epsilon fraternity. We formed a wonderful friendship that will carry on forever. Later we co-chaired our very successful tenth Andover reunion. Through the years, we have stayed in close touch. Billy has lived a life of selfless service to others.

George Streztelski was a classmate from Poland who fled Warsaw in 1939 with his mother. They moved from Paris to Milan and then to Spain. His father, a radio correspondent, joined them in Lisbon, Portugal. They lost everything. George's father contacted Ignacy Paderewski, the famous Polish pianist and politician, who helped secure them American visas and safe passage to New York. George's mother met the wife of Andover's headmaster, Claude Feuss, by chance and later called her for advice on George's educational path. As a result, after testing, he was awarded a full scholarship to Andover. George later put himself through Duke and Boston College Law School.

Frank Yatsu, another classmate, was eight when he heard on the radio that Japan had attacked Pearl Harbor. Several months later, he was told that the family was being evacuated. They were part of more than 100,000 Japanese Americans sent to relocation centers. They were transported from Los Angeles to a desert camp in Arizona that held 17,000 people. In 1944, as the war was winding down, they left and relocated to Cleveland. Frank said that the contrast between the internment camp and Andover's beautiful campus, with bright and highly motivated classmates, was a real game changer. Billy, George, and Frank all worked for their scholarships in the dining hall, called "the Beanery." Frank became the head waiter. He went on to become a world-renowned neurologist and the first Asian trustee of Brown University.

Of all the wonderful, enduring friends I made at Andover, Steve Yamamoto stands out as having a most compelling story. Steve was a third grader in Japan on December 7, 1941. Later, as a sixth grader living in Tokyo in 1944, he witnessed the massive air attacks by B-24s and B-29s from newly captured Saipan. Steve's class was evacuated to a battery manufacturing factory sixty miles west of Tokyo. They studied half the day and worked half the day in the factory. By 1945 they were moved to a remote area along the Japanese coast. Steve then moved back to a rural area west of Tokyo and enrolled in the local middle school. He was with his father for the last time when they watched a fire-bombing raid from their backyard in which over 8,000 people died. His father was killed shortly after aboard the battleship *Yamato*, sent to the bottom by the US fleet.

Steve heard of a new type of bomb dropping on Hiroshima and Nagasaki. On August 15, the family gathered in his grand-father's dining room to listen on the radio to the Emperor's recorded message saying that Japan had surrendered.

Steve went back to his former school in Tokyo in the fall. His mother got a job as a receptionist at what was to become the US embassy. On weekends, embassy personnel would use Steve's house as a home away from home. One of the staff taught at Germantown Friends School before the war and became impressed with Steve. He contacted a colleague at Germantown Friends, who had moved to Andover. As a result, Steve was awarded a full scholarship to Andover for his senior year.

Steve was oblivious to the possibility of a hostile reception in America, and he experienced none. Andover Headmaster John Kemper engaged Nat Reed, our class president, and three of us on Steve's arrival to help orient him to Andover life. In no time, Steve was buzzing around Andover with the rest of our classmates.

For our sixtieth reunion, Steve was unable to travel and asked me, as class secretary, to convey to classmates his message of gratitude for their kindness and friendship during his year at Andover, an auspicious beginning to his life in the United States and Japan. Steve received a full scholarship from Yale and eventually earned his PhD in Physics summa cum laude. Steve did his thesis on Atomic Physics.

So many of us arrived at Andover in 1947 from homes where life progressed at a far different pace than our friends', who had backgrounds we could hardly understand or appreciate at the time. The fact that they were classmates enriched us and, over time, made us realize how fortunate we had been.

—

After college, Ken and I served together as officers on the destroyer USS *Abbot* (DD-629), with two proud parents and one proud grandfather cheering us on at every turn. Had it not been for a broken leg and dislocated ankle with the loss of fifteen degrees of motion in my right ankle (from skiing on leave in Davos, Switzerland), I most probably would have stayed in the Navy. A couple of memorable events stand out from my time in the service.

The year was 1956. The USS *Abbot* (DD-629) was scheduled to begin anti-submarine warfare exercises in the Atlantic, off Bermuda, with a convoy of replenishment ships. The sea grew angrier as we moved south from Newport, Rhode Island. A hurricane had been tracking lazily north, northwest from the Caribbean, changing direction without notice. Not by design, we were heading directly for it. No matter what course we tried, the storm seemed to counter, until we were being pounded.

I was the officer of the deck on the 4:00 to 8:00 p.m. watch. I had relieved Gene McGovern, the operations officer. Next to the captain, W. W. DeVenter ("WWD" to us), Gene was second-best ship handler aboard. Gene had been on the bridge for ten straight hours. WWD had moved to his sea cabin, just aft of the bridge, as the sea conditions worsened. He spent most of the time seated in his swivel chair located in the most forward part of the wheelhouse, where he had an unobstructed view over the bow.

We were operating with seven other destroyers, a squadron consisting of two divisions of four ships each. The squadron commander, with the rank of captain, was located on the lead destroyer. We were arrayed in a line with proper spacing between the eight of us.

A Fletcher-class destroyer has a break, an open space, on the main deck amid ship between the superstructures fore and aft. Both are linked one level above by an open deck connecting the two superstructures, known as the 01 level. The only protected access from bow to stern was below the main deck. The sea state was so treacherous that WWD ordered the water-tight doors connecting the below-deck spaces dogged down.

Only men in the forward sections of the ship had sheltered access to the bridge. For twenty hours, the men quartered in the aft part of the ship, mainly engineers, had no access to the bridge and were relegated to their spaces with no hot food. Movements on the main and 01 decks were out of the question.

Ted Karras was boatswain of the watch, directing the men standing watch: lookouts, helmsman, lee helmsman, quartermasters, radioman, and back-ups. I had the con, the responsibility for running the ship. The captain was either on the bridge or in earshot of the activity in his sea cabin. The squadron commander, located on the lead destroyer, gave directions for course and speed. We were third in line, heading straight into the waves. I was braced in the open shell door leading to the starboard wing of the bridge. The ship was climbing mountainous seas and then crashing down to the troughs. We were steering 040 degrees, and our speed was twelve knots.

Crackling over the radio came the order, "Change course,

come to 130, speed fifteen knots." I grabbed the mic and acknowledged receipt of the order, and repeated the order to the helmsman and the lee helmsman. "Right full rudder, come to course 130. Make turns for fifteen knots."

The captain was in his sea cabin. He came racing forward to the wheelhouse. Ted announced, "The captain is on the bridge." WWD came bursting through the shell door past me and moved to the outer end of the open starboard wing of the bridge to assess the sea state, just as we were slowly coming to the new heading.

The order never should have been given. We were lumbering into the trough, now parallel between two huge waves. We were thrown over on our side. I lost my grip on the knife-edge of the shell door and hurtled out as the ship rolled steeply to starboard, piling onto the captain who was clinging to the alidade (a navigational device), which was bolted to the deck on the outer part of the starboard wing of the bridge.

We held on side by side as the ship continued to roll farther and farther until it seemed like we could reach down and touch the boiling sea reaching up to us. It was angry and black, fizzing like a glass of Guinness first poured. Finally, we stopped. The ship shivered and shook. We laid there for what seemed an eternity. Slowly, ever so slowly, we began to come back. We had come within five degrees of capsizing.

We later learned that we had rolled 63 degrees, "five degrees from no return." Had we not been properly ballasted, this story might never have been written. A capsizing angle calculation, called the righting moment, takes into account the ship's center of gravity and ballast. At 68 degrees we would have had it!

WWD screamed over the roar of the sea, "I have the con," relieving me on the spot. As we continued to recover, he inched his way into the wheelhouse and gave orders to return us to a course heading into the waves, at the same time adjusting speed to enable us to maneuver more easily in the treacherous seas.

He grabbed the radio mic, communicating the orders from

the squadron commander and bellowed into it, "What are you doing? Are you trying to sink us? I'll take care of my ship. We are steering independently and suggest you do the same until we work out of this."

He slammed the mic back into its cradle. We resumed our course. The violent motions of the ship became less severe.

"Mr. Rider has the con."

The engineer on watch was bleeding profusely, blood spurting from a gash on the right side of his neck. Ted and WWD were trying to undo the metal chest plate fastened around his neck that had been thrust upward when the ship had rolled and he had been thrown through the shell door. The wire connecting the speaker on the metal plate to the power source had snapped taut, causing the cut. They finally freed him. Two sailors took him below for repairs, a total of twenty-one stitches. The gunnery chief broke four ribs when he was thrown against a bulkhead in the chief's quarters, and one of the seamen in my division, off watch, suffered a concussion when he fell and banged his head on a table in the mess hall. We and the next two destroyers behind us took water down our stacks.

No one aboard that day will forget that hour and what almost happened. Ted and I had more than a bird's-eye view of the adventure. WWD was never reprimanded for disobeying orders, and we all lived to tell the tale. WWD was much loved and admired by the entire crew. His actions that day added to his legacy. He had survived Pearl Harbor as an ensign taking a destroyer to sea in the midst of the Japanese attack, and he was on the bridge of the battleship Arkansas on D-Day. He told us later that surviving that storm was as memorable as anything that he had experienced in his career.

At the farewell dinner of our ship's reunion in 2018, held on Cape Cod, Ted Karras and I were presented with framed copies of "Five Degrees from No Return," including a large schematic of what 63 degrees looks like, produced for us by shipmate Dave

Rodgers. The caption reads, "The Day God Held Our Fate in His Hands!"

We spent early January 1957 anchored off Cannes, France, much of my free time spent ashore with my brother Ken and shipmates, a well-deserved break. We had spent all but a few days at sea since leaving Newport on November 6.

We put back to sea and joined units of the 6th Fleet and Allied Navies conducting extended anti-submarine warfare exercises, plane guarding for the carrier USS *Coral Sea*, and convoy replenishment drills. At the completion of our duties, we proceeded to Beirut, Lebanon, for a five-day stay alongside the largest pier in the harbor. Joining us was the USS *Hale*, another destroyer in our division. The pier accommodated both of us on the left side. We were first in and closest to shore.

The five-day stay proved to be anything but routine. I had duty the first night. My brother and several others went into town. At breakfast the next morning, the topic centered around the Kit Kat Club and the belly dancer, reportedly the best in the Eastern Mediterranean.

During the night, a Russian freighter docked opposite the *Hale*, down the pier and catty-corner aft of us. The wind was blowing from their starboard quarter toward our port bow. Their stack was billowing thick black smoke, the residue collecting on our deck—the deck my guys had just swabbed. What a mess! Not a very friendly thing to do.

That night, I went ashore and headed straight for the Kit Kat Club. We had a great night, but there was no belly dancer. The next morning, Ken, assigned to the engineering department, notified me that the wind had changed direction and was now blowing in the direction of the Russian ship. He had arranged with his chief to return the favor and suggested that I go on deck and watch the fun. Full blast our guys produced even thicker black smoke, billowing and belching soot and gook that landed all over the Russian ship. Their sailors shook their fists. We waved back. Revenge was sweet!

As recreation officer, I had arranged a day outing by bus to view the ancient ruins at Baalbek, situated in the Beqaa Valley. Twenty crew members signed up. Ken joined us. Several of them purchased cases of beer for the trip, iced them in large buckets, and stowed them aboard the back of the bus. The ship's cooks supplied sandwiches. We left early from the pier and drove the eighty-five kilometers on a hilly route through the countryside to view the Roman treasure, ruins of the temples counted among the wonders of the world. I even rode a camel, much to the delight of all present.

On the return trip, the road took us close to the Syrian border. Ken and I were seated side by side in the back of the bus by the beer. The bad guys had set up a roadblock near the border and ordered our driver to stop and all of us to exit the bus. Our driver got in an argument with a scruffy local.

Ken said to me, "You're senior, you handle this. I'll guard the beer!"

Our driver, who spoke English, said, "Under no circumstances let anyone off this bus!"

I stood in the space behind him as he acted as mediator. Two more scruffy locals boarded the bus brandishing Kalashnikov rifles. The driver told me that they were after our film. Everyone had a camera. I told our guys not to stand up, and to hand over the film, but not their cameras. The locals went up and down the aisle collecting the film stripped from the cameras. That satisfied them, and they left the bus.

I was pissed about losing a whole film of pictures taken at sea and in Baalbek. Ken looked at me with a grin and produced a roll of film. In the confusion, he had removed the good one, placed it inside his shirt, and replaced it with a blank. We all chipped in when we returned and handed the driver a very good tip when we got off the bus.

The last day of our stay, we were scheduled to depart at noon. Breakfast was interrupted when the *Hale*'s skipper appeared in our ward room. Our captain excused himself, interrupting his breakfast, and he and the skipper both left abruptly. Half an hour later, over the squawk-box, we heard, "Ensign George Rider, report to the captain!"

The captain and the executive officer (XO) were seated when I arrived. They didn't waste time with lengthy explanations. The mystery of the missing belly dancer from the Kit Kat Club was solved! The *Hale*'s captain had asked our captain, WWD, for help in retrieving one of his young officers before the noon departure. The *Hale*'s officer had gone ashore the first night and endeared himself to Sophia, the gyrating star at the Kit Kat, and neither had surfaced since. To avoid undue attention on the *Hale*, he had asked WWD to help retrieve his officer.

In the middle of the explanation, 1st Class Boatswain Mate J.J. Cunningham appeared carrying two .45 pistols, extra clips, and a billy club. The XO had already contacted the local Beirut police, who had in turn found Sophia's address. I was to be in charge of the "rescue mission." J.J. had chosen the toughest sailor in the deck division to accompany us—Nick "Ski" Snigorski, six feet, four inches, and 235 pounds.

WWD told me to get in and out quickly with as little fanfare as possible. No force unless absolutely necessary. He wished us well. Ski was waiting for us on the dock. J.J. and I were armed with the .45s. J.J. handed the billy club to Ski just as two police cars screeched to a halt on the pier close to us, one marked, the second with just a driver. The three of us got in.

Twenty minutes later, after a drive through downtown Beirut, we arrived in the Arab quarter and pulled up behind the marked car carrying five uniformed police who were already taking station in front of and around an apartment house in the middle of a crowded street. The police captain spoke good English. We conferred and decided that the three of us from the *Abbot* would make the first contact. J.J. and I clicked a round into the chambers and proceeded to climb the steps of the two-story walkup with Ski close behind.

I knocked on the door. No answer. I waited and knocked again. It opened and before me was Sophia, the best belly dancer in the Eastern Med, scantily clad and looking none the worse for wear. Not so *Hale*'s errant ensign. He was seated on a large sofa to the right and behind her, in his skivvies, unshaven, and too tired to be defiant. I called him by name and told him to get dressed and come with us, that his ship was due to depart in under two hours. He replied that he had no intention of leaving and told me to "butt out." Sophia was still in the doorway.

I responded, "You're coming with us, one way or another! If you stay, think about it. You will be subject to Lebanese justice and US court-martial for desertion. Right now no charges have been pressed, and I'll overlook your first reaction. Now put your pants on, shape up, and get moving. You have five minutes." I stepped back. Sophia stepped back. The door was still open. The ensign looked bewildered and shook his head. The sight of me and J.J., with Ski towering behind us, did not go unnoticed. Slowly he got up, disappeared, and returned, buckling his belt and tucking in his shirt. He mumbled something to Sophia, kissed her, and brushed by me and J.J. Ski escorted him to the car, seating him between them in the backseat.

The police got into their car and led us back to the pier with forty minutes to spare before we departed. I accompanied the ensign to the quarter deck of the *Hale* and turned him over to their operations officer.

We returned to the *Abbot*, checked in our weapons, and prepared to go to sea. The captain later congratulated me. J.J. and Ski also were told later individually by the captain that he was very pleased at how well they had done. I never did get to see Sophia perform, but what I observed of her at her apartment, plus the state of the errant ensign, left no doubt about her abilities on and off the stage.

Following my Navy service, two of the best years of my life, I went to work for Bankers Trust in New York. In 1958, Betsy

Waskowitz and I married. We had five wonderful years. She died of reticulum cell sarcoma in 1963 at Sloane Kettering Hospital in New York after a terrific eighteen-month battle, at age twenty-nine.

My appetite for Wall Street went flat. I changed jobs several times, to Merrill Lynch, then to Mitchem, Jones, and Templeton, F. S. Smithers & Co., and Dominick and Dominick. The last three all went south. Wall Street had changed for me, from glittering boulevard to back alley.

Following Betsy's death, I took a room at the Yale Club in New York. I never spent another night in our New Canaan home. I rented it and sold it sometime later. Had it not been for my college roommates, friends, and neighbors, my life might have turned out far differently. Two months after moving into the Yale Club, my former Yale roommates Richard Haskel and Peter Meyer moved me into their apartment. Yale classmates Roger Hansen and John Kousi urged me to join the Downtown Athletic Club. I began to work out and socialize again. Dad often used to say that friendship is "the finest ship that sails." Friendship cannot be taught, forced, or mandated. When it happens, cherish it, nurture it, and hold it close. It's a gift.

The best time of my life was beginning to unfold as I worked to keep my career alive. Had it not been for Betsy's doctor, I never would have met Dorothy Crawford. He kept in close contact with me and worried over my physical and mental health. He urged me to call a nurse who worked on his floor, and he gave me her telephone number. I called. The rest is happy history. We married and along came Graham and Jenny. I also found happiness in my career again, spending my best and most memorable years on Wall Street at Morgan Stanley.

Graham married Paulette Eiden. Along came Graham Jr., Bradley, Tory, and Duncan. Jenny is an accomplished speechwriter specializing in crisis management and hovers over us like

Proud Poppy and his grandchildren (left to right):
Graham Jr., Tory, Duncan, and Bradley.

a doting hen. My joy each day since Dorothy said yes surpasses all else.

Tempering my current family joy is that the reality that exists today may forever taint the bright future we all wish for our kids. My abiding concern now is our grandchildren and the world they will inherit. The experiences of youth today are very different, but in some ways eerily similar. It is my hope that they have the same boldness and perseverance that I've seen displayed by so many of my friends and peers in this book.

FAIR WINDS AND FOLLOWING SEAS.

eleven

A Retired Architect's Dedication to World Friendship

by **William (Billy) Ming Sing Lee***

Billy was born in Shanghai, China, in 1932 and educated at Shanghai American School, Phillips Academy Andover, Yale College, and the Yale School of Architecture. He worked at I.M. Pei and Associates NYC and as a partner at various architectural firms, including Copelin and Lee Architects NYC. Billy has lectured on architectural design and planning in the US, China, and Italy. He has won prizes and recognition for architectural works. He has dedicated his life to promoting international friendship (www. MingSingLee.com).

I was born and brought up in Shanghai as the lucky son of a prominent Hong Kong movie producer. My father, T.Y. Lee, was considered one of the *Tai Pans* (tycoons) in Hong Kong. At age fifteen, I enrolled in Phillips Academy Andover, my father's alma mater, with my older brother Tommy, who later attended Amherst. I was active in sports and captained the Andover soccer team.

In 1949, with the founding of New China, my father's business collapsed for political reasons, and my family's situation changed abruptly. I was in my third year at Andover, and the school came to my rescue by granting me a full scholarship and a job washing dishes in the Beanery (dining hall).

With no home base in the US, I spent holidays and vacations with Andover classmates. The friendship and generosity of my classmates and their families had a great effect on me. I have written about my experiences and become an avid advocate of "home stays" in both the US and China.

After graduating from Yale, I worked as an architect, but I have spent the better part of my life promoting international friendship through cultural exchanges between China and the US. Obviously, my father's misfortune did not affect my confidence in people's intrinsic goodness. I recognize people's positives as well as negatives, but I emphasize their goodness. Our primary goal should be to cultivate people's intrinsic goodness. I see history as lessons to be learned, not grudges to hold forever. Andover taught us *"non sibi"* (not for oneself) and to strive for knowledge and goodness.

My international friendship programs include working with both US and Chinese governments as a founding director of the 1990 Institute and treasurer and membership director of US-China Peoples Friendship Association, South Bay chapter. Among my major projects, I spearheaded a children's art exchange between Chinese and American youngsters. Nearly one million Chinese students competed in the contest, "Art and the

Environment." The artwork was exhibited in several US museums and galleries for two and a half years. In another successful venture, I introduced jazz improvisation to the China Children's Center in Beijing.

The most magical moment I ever experienced was a morning when I arranged for a group of middle school students from Menlo Park, California, to travel to Beijing to do mural painting together with a group of Chinese students at the China National Children's Center. As the Chinese students, teachers, and their family members noticed that the American guests had arrived at the main gate, fifteen designated students started to line up in one row, and their teachers and parents gathered behind them. The American students, without instructions, instinctively walked forward and lined up in a row opposite the Chinese students, and their teachers and parents lined up behind them.

Ms. Chen, the Chinese activities director, cheerfully welcomed the American guests and suggested to the students who were going to paint together to close their eyes and stretch out their arms and walk slowly towards each other. That person whose hands they touched was to be his or her painting partner for the weekend. The students had a variety of facial expressions when they closed their eyes—some anxious, some curious, some more determined, and a few mischievous. Most adults from both sides were in awe. They, including myself, felt the magic of the moment. There is hope for peace, pure friendship, and goodwill for our future generations.

I hope this feeling will catch fire. My old friend CB Sung always encouraged me by referring to a Chinese saying: "A small spark can ignite a vast field."

---

* With contributions from George S.K. Rider, author of Chapter 10.

Twelve

The View in My
Ninth Decade

by **Steve Young**

Steve Young graduated from Middlebury College in 1960. Follow-
ing a call to the Arctic, he attended the University of Alaska, then
Harvard for a PhD while continuing to work in the Arctic. A stint
on the faculty at Ohio State at a time when libraries were burning,
tear gas was everywhere, and students worried about being shot,
convinced him that traditional academia wasn't an appropriate
environment. So he and his wife founded the Center for Northern
Studies in Vermont. CNS was deeply involved in planning for public
lands in Alaska. Later it formed the nucleus of the Northern Studies
Program at Middlebury and was one of the founding institutions
of the international University of the Arctic.

Steve has had the great good fortune of having middle age extend into his 80s. In gratitude, he is building a chapel inspired by the medieval wooden churches of Scandinavia.

It came to me some time around my eightieth birthday that my life now extends over halfway back to the Civil War. I remember once seeing a *Life* magazine article—I must have been seven or eight—with pictures of the few score remaining Civil War veterans. Someone born now might see a similar piece about ancient, grizzled World War II veterans in 2025 or so. The war whose events and attitudes permeated my own childhood is now ancient history.

I was born into the international chaos that would soon lead to the second World War. *Kristallnacht*, when the full evil of Nazism showed that it could no longer be denied, happened a month or so after my arrival, followed a year later by the invasion of Poland. One of my earliest memories is of Pearl Harbor. I was just over three years old, and I have a recollection of being at my grandparents' house in Rowayton, Connecticut. It's all pretty hazy, but there was a sense that something awful was happening, and that the adults around me were grave and fearful. I remember much more clearly the events of the next few months and years: the upper half of car headlights blacked out, blackout curtains, people getting together to listen, fearfully, to the radio. There were U-boats operating within sight of the New Jersey coast, and people were encouraged to become civilian plane spotters—they were issued manuals with silhouettes of Allied and Axis planes. And rationing! Sugar was a luxury, gasoline hoarded for special occasions, and you had to show pages of colored stamps to be able to buy necessities. I now realize that there was a very dark cloud over the first years of my life, but at the time that was all I knew, so it felt normal.

Things got better in a few years, and I remember a bunch of us kids going to my uncle's yard to ring a big, cast iron bell on V-E (Victory in Europe) Day. There was a hornet's nest in the bell, and I, the smallest kid, was the slowest to make a getaway. In those days we put a paste of baking soda on the stings; I doubt it did much good.

A few months later, on V-J (Victory over Japan) Day, there was pandemonium on the streets of Norwalk, hardly tempered by the fact that we had just unleashed the horror of the atomic bomb on the world. The sidewalks were full of revelers, and I remember stepping on an object that tinkled; it was an antique bronze sleigh bell that I kept for many years, but which has disappeared. I'd like to think that someone might find it again during a celebration of the end of our current wars. If they ever end.

My family was lucky. Only a few of my many relatives saw active duty, and none were killed or wounded. But the shadow of the war overlay everything about my early childhood, and that shadow only partially dissipated after 1945. There were the Nuremburg trials and the images of bombed-out cities and emaciated people on the newsreels shown before the main feature at the movie theaters. For years comic books centered on the war and depicted "Japs" or "Nips" as devious, undersized people with yellow skin, buck teeth, and thick glasses. Germans—"Krauts"— being Caucasian, fared marginally better. The specter of atomic warfare also emerged, and we were taught to climb under our school desks and protect the backs of our necks if a brilliant flash of light occurred. Soon the Korean police action began, and "Gooks" replaced the previous ethnic villains. Senator Joseph McCarthy demonstrated the power of a single evil man with a few followers to wreak havoc on a country and its citizens.

All sounds pretty bleak, doesn't it? I've often wondered if the gloom of World War II was unique, or if it marked the emergence of a new wartime mood. It was the first war in which mass media—in its primitive form, radio—brought instant and continuous news to the public. The carnage of earlier wars, although equally horrifying, was at a remove. News had to filter out over the course of days or weeks via newspapers and word of mouth.

Whatever their immediate effects, the longer-term fallout of wars lasts for decades, often centuries. It can be argued that the American Civil War is still being fought after more than 150 years, with no clear winner or, rather, with many obvious losers. Since World War II and its spawn, the Cold War, were "my" wars, I'm interested in trying to understand which aspects of their shadow have lingered on. Much of my life work involved the polar regions, especially the far north, and I'm going to concentrate on that, but I'll look at a few generalizations first.

I have often thought that a country that fought and won a "just" war may well suffer some subtle but long-lasting moral damage, and I think that this is evident in the United States. One could search far into history without finding a better example than World War II of a major war that pitted good against evil. Of course, the clarity of this myth of the triumph of virtue is seen to be somewhat tarnished by anyone with more than a cursory knowledge of twentieth century history. But the reality of the Holocaust trumps the various misdeeds and injustices perpetrated by the Allied powers, and, particularly, the United States. We were taught in our young days that America saved the Free World and rescued Europe from Nazism and other manifestations of fascism. We were the shining city on the hill, and the sense of American exceptionalism grew apace. It had, of course, many earlier manifestations; Manifest Destiny immediately comes to mind. That hubristic attitude has led us astray time and again over the decades. The array of disasters should have left American pretentions of virtue, nobility, and exceptionalism in tatters, but the attitude is so deeply embedded that it haunts us to this day, like a chronic disease.

At the same time, we Americans need to be aware of our enormous good fortune in living in a country of immense natural resources, separated from possible enemies by broad oceans, and easily annexed from its comparatively small indigenous population, which had been decimated and demoralized by disease and other factors. And we must never forget that a large portion of American economic growth for centuries was based on slave labor. There is indeed a rational basis for the American sense of exceptionalism, but it depends more on geography and history than any intrinsic virtue of being American.

Three areas in which World War II and its aftermath did seem to encourage progress were in American race relations, human rights, especially women's rights, and anti-colonialism in the world at large. Until recently, I had an unarticulated belief that there was some feature in the nature of being human that inexorably led to progress toward better treatment of everybody: not just people, but animals, forests, oceans, tundra, and the world in general. This was—and still tries to be for me—essentially a religious perspective: a belief in the sanctity of all life and the planet, perhaps the cosmos, that supports it. One would be naïve not to recognize that there are always counterforces—steps backward—in this rising tide. But only recently has it seemed to me that the tide may have turned, and the progress we have made may be transient and illusory. Some of the dread and horror of my childhood, World War II days, has reemerged.

When I look at these issues dispassionately, though, so much progress has been made since the mid-twentieth century that it would take more backsliding than even I fear to return to the bad old days. I can recall that my college, Middlebury, bragged that its female graduates swelled the ranks of teachers, secretaries, and nurses—the highest callings that women could aspire to, except, perhaps, motherhood. The female students, of course, generally far outshone the men academically. (The fact that they were in lockdown every night with no opportunities for even the mildest debauchery might have been significant; there was little alternative to studying.)

Legislative bodies at the state and national levels were, with few but sometimes notable exceptions, purely white and male. (I'm thinking here of Senator Margaret Chase Smith of Maine, whose lengthy and hard-fought battle with McCarthyism deserves to be better remembered. But even she attained her start in electoral politics in a special election to replace her departed husband.) It would still be decades before the Supreme Court had a female justice or an African American. Now it seems perfectly appropriate (to me, at least) for a woman to become president of the United States. It's been a tough row to hoe, though, and we've still got a good way to go. The same can be said about race relations.

In the early 1960s, I worked with a group of African American men, mostly from South Carolina, and mostly with minimal education. It was an eye-opener to learn what these people faced, day to day, every day of their lives. For example, when they drove up from the South in spring for work, they had to either drive nonstop or find families to stay with en route; they could not stay in motels. I still marvel at the way they kept their dignity—and their sense of humor—under this constant rain of disenfranchisement, contempt, and personal danger. Meanwhile we listened to Amos and Andy on the radio (the characters played by two white men) and learned in school the songs of Stephen C. Foster ("Old Black Joe"). Colleges put on minstrel shows with blackface. We went to see *Song of the South* at the movies: a lovable old black man extolled the virtues of the good old days, when he and his kin were enslaved. We've come a long way, yet we still have so far to go—and much of that journey involves rooting out attitudes that we seemed to have absorbed through the pores of our skin in the early decades of our lives.

When I was young, India and Pakistan were still under the

control of Great Britain. There were the Dutch East Indies, French Indochina, and the Belgian Congo. The long and bloody history of countries gaining their independence from colonial powers continues, and many of the new countries are still mired in internecine wars. Whether any of these countries could have emerged as peaceful societies living within natural boundaries if colonialism had not occurred, is an open question. The attitudes of the "developed world" certainly didn't help. During my childhood there was still serious talk among educated people of the "white man's burden," of the "lesser races," and the "uncivilized natives" of "darkest Africa." Some of the tribes were so primitive that the females went topless, as was attested to by the black-and-white photographs in the *National Geographic* articles we looked at so assiduously in those pre-*Playboy* days.

At some time in the mid-twentieth century, my interior life began to constellate around a love of wild country, wildlife, and people—past and present—who lived very different lives closer to nature and on far horizons in general. I dissembled a lot of this, especially to myself, through high school and college, but it emerged in a powerful way in my early twenties. I became a skilled amateur ornithologist, and I was especially interested in birds of the Arctic and the oceans. I took the iron ore train into northern Labrador and traveled with a friend to Newfoundland, where people still lived in outports close to the open sea and fished for a living. This shifted my love affair with wild places into high gear and focused it on the polar regions. A couple of years later, in 1963, Jan and I married and moved to Alaska, where I started work on a master's degree in biology.

The 1960s were a time of profound changes in Alaska and throughout the Circumpolar North, although we could mostly only guess what was happening in the huge Russian sector. The Cold War was more lukewarm after the Cuban Missile Crisis, and the military was spread widely and thickly across Alaska, Canada, and Greenland. Jan, who was raised as a Baptist, went to a church service in Fairbanks attended mostly by military and thought she had entered an enclave of the Deep South. She said that they stopped just short of handling snakes. Alaska had become a state only a few years earlier, and stores such as Sears were just beginning to alter the local economies, which had been dominated by small (and expensive) merchants.

The University of Alaska was in the midst of major upheavals related to an effort known as Project Chariot. This was a branch of the Atomic Energy Commission's Atoms for Peace initiative. The plan, supported by luminaries such as Edward Teller, was to use nuclear devices to blast a harbor into a site near Cape Thompson on the shores of the Chukchi Sea/Arctic Ocean far above the Arctic Circle. The idea created a good deal of well-founded skepticism, especially from the newly emerging environmental movement. The obvious question, of course, was: Who would use the harbor?

It was suggested by university people that a baseline study of the Cape Thompson environment before the blasts would be appropriate, since the explosions would obviously have an enormous effect on the surrounding ecosystems—as well as the people, Inupiat Eskimos, who still lived a partially nomadic lifestyle and depended on the local resources. This prospect provided an opportunity for university faculty members to participate in well-funded "big science," but left them open to attack by environmentalists and other opponents of the project as sellouts. The plot thickened when it was discovered that the wandering hunters of the surrounding tundra had extraordinarily high levels of radioactive isotopes, such as Strontium-90, in their bodies. The chain of causality proved to be that fallout from Russian above-ground nuclear tests traveled on the westerly winds and was deposited on the Alaskan tundra, building up on the slow-growing lichens on which caribou fed. The caribou were then hunted by the Inuit, who, it seemed, had an elevated risk of cancer. In any event, a major baseline study was completed, the project was shelved, to almost everyone's relief, and damaged relationships began to heal. And the University of Alaska was well on its way to becoming one of the major players in Arctic research, as it is today.

For myself, I felt only distant repercussions from all this. My first few months in Fairbanks were filled up with getting back into academia, learning to live in country that still had some basis for calling itself "the Last Frontier," and making friends who were involved in a variety of fascinating research projects, mostly field work far beyond the roads in bush Alaska. Then I got lucky: I received a graduate fellowship from the National Science Foundation. This paid me a modest stipend and gave me some funding for field work on a master of science program. And the university generously kicked in a bit extra.

My master's project was a study of the evolutionary and geographic relationships of the tundra bilberry (*Vaccinium uliginosum*), the common blueberry of the boreal and Arctic regions of the world. Field work gave me a chance to travel all over Alaska: the Aleutian Islands, Nome and many small villages in Western Alaska, and the North Slope and Barrow area. One thing was immediately evident: the military was everywhere. The most remote locations bristled with shining white domes and dish antennas, surrounded by high fences and guarded by grim-looking young men. On the other hand, in the villages and towns, life went on with relatively minor changes. Most military bases were manned by a few specialists and support personnel, who generally kept to themselves.

Change was about to arrive with a vengeance, though. For decades it had been more or less assumed that there were oil reserves in Arctic Alaska. There were bore holes for seismic work and test wells all over the North Slope and oil geologists skulking in the most isolated locations. But few Alaskans expected the enormous oil boom that began in the late 1960s and still dominates Alaskan politics and the state's economy. Some of the events of the 1970s could not have been predicted a few years earlier.

Perhaps the most far-reaching event was the Alaska Native Claims Settlement Act (ANCSA) of 1971. Huge sections of oil pipe were already arriving in Alaska when it was realized that much of the proposed pipeline route was over land that had never been ceded to any government entity by people of the native communities who lived on the land. This potential roadblock caused a flurry of activity at the state and national level, resulting in a complex body of legislation that placed most native communities in for-profit native corporations and gave them title to vast tracts of land. The act also gave the state of Alaska title to land comparable in area to one of the western states, and it sought to place much of the remaining federal lands under the aegis of the National Park Service, the Fish and Wildlife Service, the Bureau of Land Management, and the National Forest Service. The Park Service turned out to be the big winner in succeeding machinations, with the result that the area of federal land under the control of the Park Service in the US more than doubled. All of this resulted in vast changes in management regimes throughout Alaska and some very powerful backlash from Alaskans—mostly white Alaskans—who wanted to live unencumbered by the rules and regulations promulgated by governments of any sort.

Meanwhile the Cold War grumbled on. The Distant Early Warning Line, an array of sites stretching across western and northern Alaska, the Canadian Arctic, and Greenland in order to detect Russian bombers crossing the Arctic Ocean, had been made obsolete by intercontinental ballistic missiles. New technology was constantly being deployed across the Arctic. Satellite imagery was replacing aerial photography from U-2s, and the Russians were commissioning nuclear-powered icebreakers to traverse the polar seas.

I've often felt that I was lucky and just made it under the

wire to experience bush Alaska in its pristine form. I traveled hundreds of miles of Bering Sea coast in traditional walrus-skin boats, lived off the land, and explored places where few white people had been. I didn't need to worry about whose land I was on or to get collecting permits, as I would have a few years later. Drugs had not yet arrived in the native communities, although alcohol abuse was often rampant. Overall, the bush villages were good places to be, and I met and worked with some very fine people; I appreciate them even more from the perspective of fifty years. The success of my PhD research—as well as my continued survival—depended very much on the skill and judgement of the captains of the skin boats of the Bering Sea islands.

The changes taking place in the Arctic were mirrored in some way by those occurring at the other end of the world. At the end of World War II, Antarctica was still mostly *terra incognita*, largely ignored since the days of Amundsen, Scott, and Shackleton. This changed as nations began to think seriously about territorial claims and the possibility of military and economic activities in the frozen continent and the surrounding seas, which were rapidly being depleted of whales. (I understand that much of the margarine consumed in Great Britain in the immediate postwar years was derived from whale blubber.)

The first big scientific push into Antarctica was an American effort, Operation Deepfreeze, led by Admiral Richard E. Byrd. In the years that followed, Americans established a major base on McMurdo Sound, the farthest south point that could be reached by ship. There was a strong impetus, led by the United States, to create an Antarctic Treaty that would protect the continent from military and commercial development for an extended period of time but not abrogate the claims on the territory made by various countries. The byword was, "A Continent for Science." This effort has held up remarkably well over the decades, although there is a bit of sniping in the sector of the Antarctic Peninsula, where land claims of Chile, Argentina, and the UK overlap. I was present when nature took a hand in this. Each of the three claimant countries maintained a scientific base on Deception Island, a volcanic caldera off the coast of the Antarctic Peninsula. An eruption occurred, wiping out the brand new Chilean base and the British facility, while leaving the Argentine buildings untouched. I was also in the area when the first tourist ship arrived in Antarctica. Mrs. Ernest Hemingway was on board and, it was said, caught a large fish from the deck. Now the tourist industry is a major—and controversial—player in Antarctic issues, although it is mostly confined to the spectacular Antarctic Peninsula/Drake Passage sector. Most other Antarctic coasts are characterized by endless stretches of beetling ice cliffs.

When I worked in Antarctica around 1970, glaciology was a specialized and relatively unknown field. Now, of course, it is absolutely central to discussions of climate change and is in the headlines constantly. In 1970 we still thought that we were on a climatic downturn that slowly, but inexorably, would lead us into the next ice age. I once spent a week marooned in the Antarctic Dry Valleys with a Russian glaciologist. The glaciers seemed to be comatose, without any obvious activity. With Sergei's broken English and my non-existent Russian, we had some interesting discussions. I especially remember his take on the Czech uprising of 1968, which he understood to be a failed Nazi coup.

I was also in Antarctica when the first women scientists arrived—very carefully cosseted. They were marched abreast down the gangplank of a C-130 at the South Pole, so none of them could be said to be the first woman at Pole Station. I also remember traveling in the wonderful research vessel, RV Hero, which had been fitted with a special cabin with a double-locked door so that women scientists could feel safe. The cabin held four bunks, and several of us were upset for being assigned less desirable quarters in order to accommodate the one woman aboard. Fortunately in this case it was a temporary problem, since she soon moved in with the captain, and the cabin became available again.

In the 1970s there began to be thaws in the Cold War. This affected me because the XII International Botanical Congress was held in Leningrad (now St. Petersburg again) in 1975. This was the first major international scientific meeting ever held in the USSR, and the first chance many Westerners had to see Russia firsthand. It was my first of many visits to the country, and my impressions are still fresh. In many ways, it was the saddest country I have ever been to. My last visit was in 2000, and I've had little basis for changing my perception. But I have gotten opportunities to travel across the Russian Arctic, and my attitudes and respect for many of the Russians I've met have deepened considerably.

Leningrad had suffered terribly in World War II, and evidence was still everywhere, especially in the form of war memorials. Soviet policy had resulted in the construction of massive, brutalist apartment blocks everywhere. They were concrete gray, and the shoddiness of their construction was evident even from the streets. I remember thinking that it was a great mercy that the city isn't in an earthquake zone. Those hideous buildings looked as if they would have collapsed at the first tremor.

I had been encouraged by a Russian colleague to sign up for a post-congress field expedition to northeastern Siberia, but, in typical Soviet fashion, this was cancelled at the last minute with no explanation. All in all, it was a fascinating exposure to a truly strange country; I remember breathing an immense sigh of relief as the train left Soviet territory and entered Finland. The faded greens and ochres of the old Russian buildings were replaced by Marimekko colors everywhere.

As relations improved between Russia and the West, I had more opportunities to travel far into the Russian hinterlands. Yakutsk, a major city located deep in the frigid province of Sakha, had almost the appearance of a boomtown, with building cranes all over the skyline and Canadian contractors building a model village. But the residential buildings were as dank and dreary as elsewhere in Russia.

So many good things could have happened in post-Soviet Russia, and this is an area in which American hubris surely deserves some of the blame. We, and the West in general, could have lent an enormous helping hand to a country that was struggling and at a balance point. But the US as a country was so focused on having "won" the Cold War, and on humiliating a troubled former adversary, that we failed to take advantage of what could have been a new, more peaceful world order. Gorbachev had great wisdom in his comment that Russia was going to do a terrible thing to the US—deprive us of an enemy. Instead, here we are back in a reasonable facsimile of the Cold War. Perhaps it was inevitable, but it seems to me to be one of the greatest tragedies of our time. And Russia continues to spend a major portion of its limited wealth on its military, while the infrastructure collapses, all sorts of appalling environmental degradation gets worse and worse, and the main source of wealth is in extractive industries that leave environmental and social havoc behind.

One positive aspect of the fall of the Soviet Union was the independence of many Soviet satellite countries, and one of the most interesting stories associated with this process is in Mongolia, a country that was firmly closed to Westerners until 1990. When I first arrived there, as a visiting scientist and guest of Ed Nef, it had begun to blossom. New businesses were opening, cell phones were everywhere, and internet cafes provided contact with the rest of the world. Shamans, who had been persecuted—often killed—by the previous regime, were reappearing. Buddhist temples and monasteries, whose earlier inhabitants had been exterminated fifty years ago, were being refurbished. Of course the bleak monuments of Soviet times were still around, and the transition to a modern society wasn't always smooth, but one immediately sensed that Mongolia was on the move. It was a very different sense than I had encountered in Russia, whose border was close by to the north.

The last time I was in wilderness Alaska, in the Brooks Range and Noatak Valley in 2013, change was evident in all sorts of subtle, and sometimes obvious, ways. We had a luxurious camp on the shores of Feniak Lake, where I had set up a field camp in 1973. We had moved to a different location, because the original site, although under the aegis of the National Park Service, was subject to some overlapping native claims. In 1973 we were supplied by a float plane we chartered from Kotzebue, which came in every week or so and brought us food and news. Now we had a satellite telephone system that allowed us to call anywhere in the world in seconds.

I had been invited along as a consultant by my colleague and former student, Dr. Andrew Balser, and our project had use of a helicopter. Plenty of extra time had been factored in in case of bad weather, as was wise and traditional in the Arctic. However, the weather was perfect, warm and sunny. Most of the scientists finished up their work in a couple of days and spent the rest of the time fishing for lake trout, which congregated near the outlet of the stream feeding the lake. So we had the helicopter pretty much at our disposal for several days. I remembered so many places that I'd seen from the window of a Cessna 185 over forty years earlier and wondered about. The tundra, which may look monotonous from ground level, is infinitely varied when seen from the air. Now all we had to do was ask the pilot to land, and we could check out whatever intriguing thing we saw.

No one who has spent time in the Arctic over several decades can conscientiously downplay climate change; the evidence is overwhelming. With the thawing of permafrost, the land is literally disintegrating before our eyes. In the Brooks Range, we saw that mudflows were turning portions of the tundra into gray, muddy slumps. Tall shrubs and even trees were encroaching on what had been tundra grasslands and sedge meadows. Along the Siberian coast, huge areas of ice-rich terrain are being undercut by the sea, and Greenland, of course, is in the process of diminishing its ice cap. Even Antarctica is being affected, and the eternal ice may be less eternal than we thought. In the mountains of the temperate regions, glaciers are shrinking everywhere, their loss threatening water supplies in areas as far removed from each other as Norway, Peru, and India. One unexpected feature of this waning of the glaciers has been the uncovering of a treasure trove of archaeological material, ranging from hunting implements to the frozen body of Ötzi the Iceman, high in the Alps.

I am convinced, as a scientist, that climate change will be seen to be the defining issue of the time when my grandchildren will be in charge of the earth. Of course, this can't really be separated from other problems. If the world had only half or a quarter as many human beings as it has now, climate issues would be much more manageable, even minimal. And the effects of climate change are already making huge inroads into our lives in both direct and indirect ways. Wildfires in California, island erosion in North Carolina, flooding in the middle of the continent, and hurricanes of increased power and duration are all obvious results. Migrations of people from drought- or flood-stricken regions are less obviously the direct results of climate change, but it's clearly a factor.

I hope that, a lifetime from now, we will be remembered as the generation that woke up to the realities of climate change with its clear danger to civilization and began to do something about it. I wish I could be more confident that we'd deserve the honor.

Thirteen

Military and Arctic Diversions

by Ed Nef

Ed Nef, a former diplomat, entrepreneur, and documentary film producer, has led a far-flung life of service and adventure. He turned his success operating foreign language schools into a family foundation that funded twenty-two projects in nine countries. A former part-time flight instructor and an accomplished sailor, Ed lives with his wife, Elizabeth, in Northern Virginia.

The early 1940s shattered the world; the mid and late 1940s started its reconstruction. The mid 1950s witnessed my military services with the US Army and my maturation. This was followed by twenty-five years of government service, especially in the Foreign Service, which eventually presented me with a fascinating view of the Arctic regions of the world.

As an eight-year-old in 1941, I remember little except the eternally fresh single memory of returning home from a Sunday family outing on December 7 to be greeted by the elevator man (we lived in a New York City apartment) with an ashen face and fright in his eyes.

"Have you heard?" he blurted out.

"No," we said.

"We are at war."

All I remember of the rest of the evening is the sudden hushed and shocked murmur of my parents, their opening the apartment door and rushing to turn on the radio, their frantically calling family and friends, all the while trying not to frighten my sister and me.

She and I tried to steer clear but at the same time wanted very much to know what was going on. We asked questions; answers were given sadly and quickly. No one really knows, they said. And the next morning, we must have been escorted to school per family routine, but I admit to having little memory of what happened in school—or at home—in the ensuing days. I'm sure teachers and parents tried to remain calm and authoritative, and they probably succeeded after a while, which is why childhood memories of the war are scarce.

I clearly remember the end of the war. 1945 was the critical year—on May 8 came the end of European hostilities, with Japan's surrender several months later. It's hard to pinpoint exactly when all fighting ended, since there was sporadic Japanese guerilla warfare for a long time. All the tumult and excitement of victory was also spread out: the wild, Times Square partying in New York City, the parades, the cheers on the first day, and further celebrations lasting more than one or two days all over the continent.

We children were aware that tumultuous events were taking place, but we quickly adapted to the changing scene. We accepted many new things: the end of food rationing, the sudden availability (important to children) of chocolate and candy, and gasoline for car travel. Yet everyone slowly became more and more anxious as the Soviets proceeded to seal off Eastern Europe and eventually lower the Iron Curtain. This was a truly poignant and sad time for us, especially for my mother. She had longed for peace so she could reunite with her family in Poland, which had suffered so much while under German domination. Instead it was impossible to visit Poland. She eventually succeeded in visiting briefly, but only because my father was a Swiss diplomat and she carried a Swiss diplomatic passport.

Despite that, and just as important for our family, was the possibility to take family vacations and travel freely in Western Europe. By 1946 we readied for the first family "adventure." This was to take one of the newly scheduled transatlantic flights to Europe to visit family in Switzerland. We flew in what was then a brand-new means of international transportation: a *huge* (to us) DC-4 that lumbered across the Atlantic unpressurized, which meant flight at 8,000 feet and quick landings when weather was bad. After taking off from LaGuardia Airport in May in the early afternoon, we landed in Gander, Newfoundland, after a six-hour flight for a scheduled refueling stop. We ended up spending some ten hours there because of bad weather over the Atlantic.

Once we took off from Gander, we had some very bumpy flying, which fortunately did not bother us—none in the family ever had any motion sickness—but still it was slow going. Next stop was Shannon, Ireland, for breakfast, then Paris for lunch, and finally our destination, Geneva, Switzerland, where we were to spend a few days. In all, the journey from LaGuardia to Geneva consumed at least forty hours.

An explanation here: My father was the Swiss consul general in New York, and, not surprisingly, his government wanted him to come back to Switzerland for consultations as soon as possible after hostilities ended, particularly because the Swiss government had recently named him the first Swiss ambassador to Canada. Switzerland had played a very important role in the war; the country had remained staunchly neutral and thus had been called upon to communicate among all parties. So the trip was not a vacation for Dad, but my parents always wanted to go everywhere as a family, so we tagged along. That of course was great for my sister and me.

The US had saved Europe and Asia, even though both stood in 1945 much destroyed, their infrastructures seriously damaged, their economies shattered. The losers were totally dispirited, and those who were friendly to the US (almost everyone in the Western world) were glad to take on the mantle of victors alongside us. We were amazingly good-natured and felt sorry for those Allies of ours, who now had to face the monumental task of reconstruction.

We didn't try to take anyone over, including the Germans, and instead worked to bring back prosperity to the world. We gave generously to all, including the Germans. The only fly in the ointment was the Soviet Union. Many Americans hailed them as fellow victors, so it was a deep disappointment when fairly rapidly we found ourselves in the Cold War with the Russians. The Berlin Wall was built by them to totally separate the two spheres of influence. We found ourselves isolated from countries we had long considered peaceful and friendly such as Poland, Czechoslovakia, and the rest of Eastern Europe.

One of the truly inspirational events was the famed Berlin Airlift in the late forties. The Soviets would not allow land transit to Berlin but could not stop air traffic. For months, the Allies mounted a nonstop airlifting of food and supplies to Berlin until the Soviets finally gave up the effort. Meanwhile, we let dangle the other countries taken over by the Soviets, such as Poland. This was obviously enormously painful to my mother.

The US military hunkered down and took an armed defensive stance, which meant a long-term commitment of the US military to the defense of the Western world. This was indeed a very radical change in the American perspective. We couldn't look meek and mild; we had to protect the West. The Soviets had gobbled up all of Eastern Europe, imposed its dictatorships on those unfortunate lands, and poured troops and armaments into the countries they had seized. We in turn built up our troops and expected a long tenure defending against Soviet encroachment.

Very quickly my generation began to sense the pressure to grow up, to accept all the responsibilities that went with the country's new focus on the Cold War. A big change for me was moving from a relatively unfettered primary school existence to high school. Significant events were aptitude tests and entrance examinations to determine acceptance at the school of first, second, third or more choice. Classes all day, mixed with some interesting and fun sports participation. Homework in the evenings.

More stressful when I entered tenth grade was the decision by my parents and me that boarding school was the next step. For the first time in my life, I was leaving home for periods of several months' duration. No paternal supervision, just stern housemasters. I was on my own and admittedly considerably homesick at first. My parents were very proud, since the top-level boarding schools in the US such as Phillips Academy Andover (mine) were very prestigious, provided the best education, and were not so easy to get into. I'm not sure I shared their positive view.

During those school years, the US entered new hostilities in Korea. My generation suddenly had to face the reality of going to war. Our leaders established a draft to be sure all young American men would serve in the military. When the Korean War started, there was great patriotic zeal, with individuals rushing down to enlist. By my time four years later, enlisting was viewed simply as a not-very-popular civic responsibility.

My father every now and then suggested that my Swiss citizenship (I had dual nationality, born of Swiss parents in the US) could be used to keep me out of the military. I categorically rejected the idea, and my folks quietly accepted my decision. Both my parents were profoundly pro-American. At age eighteen, as a freshman at Harvard, I went down to the Selective Service office as required and duly signed up for the draft. I opted for the shortest enrollment—two years in the Army. At the same time, I claimed my student deferment, which was granted without any hesitancy. Thus, I could be reasonably assured of four more years of freedom.

By the time I graduated, Korea was winding down. The diminished patriotic fervor was quite evident, and informal conversation revolved around how to keep a deferment. This resulted in a great growth of popularity for grad schools. I mildly disapproved; I thought we had a civic responsibility to serve. In Switzerland, all men had to serve in the military upon reaching eighteen, and I thought that was a good idea.

After my graduation in 1955, there was a period of uncertainty, not knowing when I would be called up by the draft. I was very fortunate that family contacts with the Swiss business community ended up providing me with a brief internship with the Nestlé Corporation. From my point of view, it was ideal—learn a bit about business in one of the world's largest corporations while waiting for the draft to summon me onward.

Inevitably, one fine day during my internship I received a letter stating, "Greetings! You have been selected . . . ," which was the way the Selective Service chose to tell you your time had come. I had to report for duty in September 1956.

I returned home to Ottawa to pack my bag and prepare myself for going to war, should that happen. No one thought it would, but it gave purpose to my stride when my folks drove me down to the border. From Ogdensburg, New York, I caught a train to Syracuse, where I and several other morose-looking young men gathered by the railroad track.

Things moved rapidly after that. First, Syracuse, where we all filled out lots of paperwork and were duly sworn in. Then back on a train and off to Fort Dix, New Jersey, our first contact with the real Army. There we all received buzz haircuts and were issued uniforms, clothing, and boots—the essentials. Lots of rushing around, sergeants yelling at us, and sleeping in a barracks with some thirty other recruits in bunk beds. Obviously, we were no longer at home.

I enjoyed forming first friendships. What nice guys rural Americans turned out to be. I was drafted in a part of the US mostly populated by farm folk and small-town people—northern New York across the border from Ottawa, where my parents lived. Many had heavy rural accents. We happened to end up in the same basic training units, and we remained friends for a long time. We had fun in a weird sort of way—after all, we were being trained as killers—and it made the whole experience much more palatable.

They had good senses of humor, usually quite colorful and a bit raunchy, but that was part of the fun. My education sure was broadened for the better. We were all bound by an underlying common purpose: We were there to be ready to defend the country, even though we never spoke of that and rarely thought about it. I never would have had similar experiences otherwise.

At one point in advanced infantry training, a whole group of new recruits joined us from New York City, my place of birth. But these guys were so different; they talked about time in jail, about times so wild on the streets I wondered how they had survived.

My fellow rural recruits and I stuck together and did our best to ignore the newcomers. I tried to pretend I was a country boy, not one of those woebegones from urban USA.

Time passed quickly and exhaustingly. I can't say it was so easy. Awakened between 4:00 a.m. and 5:00 a.m., or even occasionally earlier, by a screaming sergeant, dressed in a hurry, out to the mess hall to chow down, and onto the parade field with our weapons (M-1 rifles). Then we might march several miles to a designated training area, which could be a huge firing range, to familiarize ourselves with all sorts of weapons, from .45-caliber hand weapons to submachine guns, hand grenades, etc. We also heard lectures on map reading, hand-to-hand combat, and more.

I'll always remember bayonet training. "What's the spirit of the bayonet?" a sergeant would yell. Then, thrusting forward with our bayonet-equipped rifle, we would respond loudly in unison, "To kill!" I don't think it made any of us murderers, since we did think the drill was monotonous and uninspiring.

This went on for some twelve weeks. After the initial few weeks, we were allowed off base for a weekend if we passed a rigorous inspection. That was nice but a bit disappointing; none of us knew the Fort Knox, Kentucky, area (where we were sent from Fort Dix for our basic training). I did become friends with another recruit who dreamed of becoming a pilot. On one of our first weekends, he invited me to tag along as he went to the nearby rural airport to see the planes and talk to the locals.

One of the pilots hanging around the hangar learned of our interest in flying and, seeing we were in uniform, invited us for a quick flight. Patriotism was still real, and we thought that was so nice of him. It was the first time I flew in a small plane, and it had an impact on me, as I soon became a flying enthusiast.

So this was my introduction to the military. It was not particularly pleasant. I was compelled to do lots of things I never really contemplated doing, from cleaning latrines to peeling potatoes.

Worst of all were the rigorous physical training, constant harass-
ment by sergeants, little sleep, and playing war. But when basic
training concluded, it was off to do what the Army decided I
would do for the remaining two years of service.

I went to Signal School in Fort Monmouth, New Jersey, to
learn how to repair telephones and repeater equipment. This
was known as the country club of military training centers, since
the studies were basically technical and obviously not physically
stressful. In fact, there was a critical shortage of soldiers with
such training (the military occupational specialty or MOS, as
the Army called it), and we were put into night school, which
sounded pretty good to me. Reveille at 4:00 p.m., classes until
11:00 p.m., lights out at 1:00 a.m., for four months. It was close
to New York City and many friends, with weekends usually free.
What was there not to like, given the circumstances?

The day came when this training ended, and we were about to
embark on the real life of a soldier. Orders came down sending
many of us, including me, to the 34th Signal Battalion in Stuttgart, Germany. We traveled by troopship to Europe. I recall the
great unhappiness of most of my fellow GIs as we were crammed
into holds filled with bunks three or four levels high. When the
sea was rough, it really could be uncomfortable (I always grabbed
a top bunk).

In Germany, we were part of the communications system
of front-line troops who were mostly infantrymen, tankers,
machine-gunners, and others who would do the fighting and
dying. All that meant for us was that we would spend our days
fixing telephone equipment. But, once again, fate intervened.
As I checked into my new home, Company E of the 34th Signal
Battalion, the receiving sergeant looked me over and, after a
moment's reflection, asked me if I could type.

"Yes, sir," I replied.

"Sorry," he said. "I'm going to have to put you in Headquarters

Company to handle our financial clerk work." I may have pretended to look crestfallen, but in reality I could hardly conceive of a better onward assignment.

Occasionally, work could get interesting. One day while on maneuvers, the door to the quarters where we had been billeted burst open and a young second lieutenant ran in, pointed his finger at me, and said, "You have just been shot. Lie down and await evacuation."

I did as I was told, and a few moments later some troops carrying a stretcher arrived. The second lieutenant pointed at me, the troops grabbed my belongings, put me on the stretcher, and rushed me out the door to a field just behind our barrack location. They lifted me up very unceremoniously and shoved me in the door of a waiting helicopter. Several other troops were already in there, including some friends. Then, whishhhh! Off we soared.

A very short ride later, the helicopter flew over a big red cross—a field hospital—before settling to earth. The copter's door flew open, new troops grabbed my stretcher (with me obviously hanging on for dear life), and rushed into the hospital. A very serious nurse greeted us, and, after a quick glance at me, ordered that they take me into the emergency room. I was beginning to wonder how far they would go with this! I was placed on an operating table, and everyone disappeared.

I wasn't alone for long. The nurse and her stretcher bearers reappeared and proceeded to rush me out the door. "No, no! Stop. Take him out head first!" the nurse screamed. I guessed that taking someone out feet first meant they were dead. They took me to the hospital ward where I was dumped on a bunk. I was handed sheets and told to remain near my bunk until further notice. There I was with a whole bunch of other troops who had gone through similar drills.

I rarely saw any supervisors. We were on our own to find the hospital mess hall and free to pass the time any way we wished. Finally, on the third day, an officer appeared and told us to get

*Those are Ed's boots sticking out of a stretcher as
he was "evacuated" to the Army field hospital.*

our gear together and head back to our home barracks, which was
maybe a thirty-minute drive away. Maneuvers had ended. Trucks
were buzzing around, and it was up to us to find one headed our
way. We finally hitched a ride, and not too long after we were safe
and sound in our home barracks. End of adventure.

In the following months, life was pretty routine. I had a good
bunch of friends, and work was fairly leisurely, with plenty of
leave time allowing frequent trips to interesting places. My buddies and I visited most of Western Europe, from Scandinavia to
Spain and Italy. My sister, Irene, who was living and working in
Madrid (her husband was the UPI bureau correspondent there)
invited me to visit for Christmas.

The life of occupying US forces could be nice. Gasoline was

subsidized (twenty-five cents a gallon) by the government for its personnel, and all the big resorts had special luxury hotels reserved for US troops (for two dollars a night). This was also a time when Europe, including Germany, was beginning to bask in new prosperity, and sports cars were very, very popular.

My time in Germany began to wind down, and I counted the days until it was my turn to rotate out, get on a train to Bremer-haven, and sail home. As my troop ship made its way across the Atlantic to the US, something went very wrong. Suddenly, the ship began a big maneuver. It was making a 180-degree turn and heading back to Europe.

At that time, the Cold War was acting up. There were serious threats being tossed across the East-West border in Germany, and Lebanon had become a hot spot. There were about 1,500 troops on the ship, and all of us couldn't believe what was hap-pening. Our releases were surely being postponed, and we were headed back to the East-West border to prepare for true military confrontation. Panic!

Thank goodness, it was a false alarm. Since our ship had medi-cal services on board, all we were doing was going back about two hours to rendezvous with a civilian ship where a crew member had been injured in an explosion on board. Our ship would give him the medical services he needed.

After that scare, we had a stretch of rough seas for a day or two. I was rewarded for my apparent immunity to seasickness by getting assigned to latrine duty. This meant standing by the entrance to the latrine with a mop and having to clean the terrain whenever some poor seasick GI didn't make it to the toilets. Ah, the joys of military discipline.

On August 13, 1958, I was once again a civilian.

I think almost all of us, once back in civilian life, began to look on those two or more years of military service as some of the most interesting and valuable times in our lives. We learned so much about our fellow Americans, who we otherwise would never

*Mike Dow, author of Chapter 3,
and Ed skiing in Europe.*

have met or known, and that was an incredible bit of learning. It humbled us and made us appreciate the world we lived in and the richness of our societies. From the wealthiest to the poorest, we were all thrown together and found that much could be learned from each other. I felt sorry for those who missed the experience.

We also learned so much about jobs we might otherwise never have come across—from kitchen scullery work to guard duty to weapons maintenance. I'm rather proud that I learned how to repair telephone equipment, a skill I otherwise wouldn't have even attempted, during my four-month training cycle at Fort Monmouth.

When my Army buddy Mike Dow and I communicated again after fifty-nine years, he told me he considered his Army career one of the most interesting and valuable experiences of his life.

Like me, Mike became interested in aviation. As we grew older, we both got involved in helping the less fortunate. Mike headed up a foundation operating under the Dow wing, while I set up my own family foundation.

While I was in the service, I did not like it, and I grumbled interminably. But from the moment I got out, I looked back on the experience as one of the best of my life. In many ways, it made me grow up and accept my fate more philosophically. I learned a great deal about my country and about the fascinating mix of wonderful people who populate it. I learned how life is not so easy for many, and that has made me eternally sympathetic to the less fortunate.

I learned the importance of discipline and to suck it up when things didn't go my way. They were important qualities, it turned out, that I would need in abundance after I began my career in the US Foreign Service. They were also particularly valuable when I went into the private sector on my own.

———

Looking back, my two-year military service was a perfect beginning to my decades-long public service career. Soon after my return to the United States, I became a Foreign Service Officer at the State Department. For me, the highlight of my subsequent twenty-five-year government career, mostly in the Foreign Service, was working in the Arctic.

From 1972 to 1976, I was assigned to the US embassy in Ottawa as a political officer. One of my responsibilities was to report on the Arctic region. This assignment appealed to me in a couple of ways. As an experienced pilot, I liked the idea of flying in very remote frozen areas, often inaccessible except by aircraft. I also had great interest in the Arctic as a prime area of potential conflict with an ever-threatening Soviet Union. The US government was nervous about these neighbors to the north and over the Pole and wondered how vulnerable we would be to encroachments by them.

An enormous amount of money was spent in the late fifties to construct the DEW (Distant Early Warning) Line, a series of radar stations all across the barren, frozen Canadian and US north manned by radar technicians and others. This was a very lonely and remote assignment for those stationed there: six months of darkness in winter (temperatures often fifty degrees below freezing), and six months of relative warmth (maybe thirty degrees) and twenty-four-hour daylight.

Along with the construction of the DEW Line, the 1957 North American Air Defense Agreement placed the Air Forces of Canada and the United States under joint command. Its name was later changed to the North American Aerospace Defense Command, but it kept the NORAD acronym. My duties were varied, from being sent as escort officer for large US Congressional delegations traveling to the Arctic, to serving as liaison to the oil companies exploring and exploiting for the first time the north's vast natural resources.

Equally important as the DEW Line was the construction of the trans-Alaska pipeline (1975–1977), built to supply the lower forty-eight with the huge quantities of oil discovered off the north coast of Alaska around Prudhoe Bay. It was an enormous undertaking to drill for and exploit oil discovered deep in the Arctic Ocean under tons of ice and then build hundreds of miles of oil pipeline. The pipe had to span the entire state of Alaska, down to the Pacific, and across open plains, high mountain ranges, and frozen rivers.

Although the Arctic is a barren place, huge herds (hundreds of thousands) of animals survive and thrive by marching across the north, seeking seasonal changes in edibles and temperature. Such a huge, human-built pipeline, ten to twenty feet high and hundreds of miles long, could block caribous' migratory passage, potentially killing entire herds.

This issue was hotly debated. The pipeline people argued the herds would figure something out; the environmentalists called this wishful thinking. To the credit of both sides, they agreed to try an experiment. For every few miles of pipeline, they would construct land bridges up and over it. Would it work?

Everyone waited and watched tensely for the arrival of the first herds. Apparently, they all came to a screeching halt when they reached the pipeline. Then, gingerly, a few sniffed the bridges, pawed the ground, and inched their way up, over, and down the other side. Then they lowered their heads and went on their way. The rest slowly followed. Hallelujah.

My first visit to the Arctic was to Prudhoe Bay in northern Alaska, the headquarters for the large oil exploration and construction underway at the time. It was a huge, open space frozen solid with snow and ice, a forbidding scene particularly in the darkness of night. In daylight, the snow would shimmer and glisten, the sky was often light and blue (in summer), and the air was clear and clean.

It was a fairly large community composed of numerous buildings linked by heated passageways. There were dormitories, a small hotel, recreation halls, a large dining hall, and a landing strip—a whole little community living unto itself. Everything inside was heated and comfortable.

If a plane landed or took off, it could not turn off its engine until it had been stored in a heated hanger. If left outside for even a few minutes, it would freeze and become useless. If you chose to walk around a bit, Arctic clothing was extremely bulky, but it did keep you warm as long as you kept moving.

The local population, ranging from native people to radar and other technicians, were gracious in showing me their exploratory wells, oil rigs, and storage silos. They even took me on short flights around the area. One time I hitched a ride on a plane used to fly supplies and individuals to and from our bases in the north country. I was returning from a visit to Dawson, Alaska, a major terminal for the Alaska pipeline. The pipeline had become so controversial; we were encountering considerable criticism from the Canadians, mostly on environmental matters, and the embassy had wanted an update. The plane was a military DC-3, very informal, with the pilot cabin door open. We weren't more than eight or ten passengers. As a pilot, I naturally hung around the cabin and eavesdropped, which they didn't seem to mind. I looked out the window and noticed a thin layer of ice accumulating on the wing; the pilot evidently noticed it at the same time, for the wing de-icers were suddenly at work. These are like large rubber balloons attached to the leading edge of the wing. When turned on, the balloons quickly start to inflate, theoretically causing the ice accumulation on the wing to crack and break off.

This worked at first, but one could see the battle was being lost. Ice accumulated faster than the deicers removed it. The pilot radioed anxiously to air traffic control and requested a change of altitude where the temperature would work for us by warming the wing. Permission was immediately granted, and the pilot went to work, playing with the deicing equipment and making the plane do some dancing up and down.

Suddenly, I could see large slabs of ice quickly sliding off the wing. The plane regained stability, and in a few moments we burst out of the clouds and into sunshine. You could hear a muffled sigh of relief and praise for the pilot. I learned that such occurrences were not unusual in this new environment; you had to live with it. For all the inherent risk, I must confess that nothing moved my romantic heart so much as flying in the Arctic at night beneath a star-filled sky. Occasional shooting stars appeared. The vast and empty snow-covered landscape of plains and high mountains lay below. The only sound was the muffled purr of the aircraft engine.

One of my greatest joys was the result of my good fortune to be a licensed pilot and flight instructor. When taking off on a trip across the Arctic in a small aircraft—mostly single-engine,

four-to-six-passenger craft—the pilot in charge might ask if anyone on board was also a pilot. "And how!" I would practically
bellow. I would be designated copilot *pro tem* and fly the plane in
this winter wonderland. The memory remains with me forever.

There are a number of stories about the Arctic that can curl
your hair. One particularly tragic story was impossible to forget.
A rescue pilot was dispatched from one of the northern stations
to a remote corner where a woman was having severe labor pains
and needed to be evacuated to a hospital. He picked her up in
his plane and started to fly back to his base on the DEW Line.

Unfortunately, as often happens up there, the weather turned
very nasty very quickly. Soon the pilot found himself in the midst
of snow and ice. The plane crashed. He survived, but she was
severely injured and died. Home base sent out search planes as
soon as the weather permitted, but several days of fruitless efforts
resulted in no success, and eventually the search was called off.
The assumption was that they had both been killed.

For three months the pilot survived alone in his wrecked
airplane in the middle of the frozen terrain of the Arctic. He had
supplies that lasted him a while, but eventually he had nothing.
He could melt ice to drink but had no food for sustenance. So
he ate parts of his passenger. It was either that or die. This sounds
like a horrible choice, and indeed it was, but one must consider
the environment.

The local native population had long ago accepted cannibalism as a necessary fact of life if one wanted to survive. They had
been doing it over centuries. They understood the powerful need
to survive and how horrible death in the Arctic could be. For a
Western-raised and educated person to resort to the practice
was a horrible repudiation of everything he had been taught, an
incredibly brave and countercultural thing to do.

I was visiting the DEW Line station when I heard of the
missing pilot. These stations were remarkably isolated and lonely
places. You could see them easily: a big, round radar dome on

top of a small cluster of buildings and, not too far off, a landing strip. Then vast, open spaces. Most of the stations were on Canadian territory, built by the US and manned by personnel from both countries. It was imperative that US officials such as I keep track of them by visiting once in a while. They were linked by modern technology and communications, so when an accident occurred, the DEW Line station could act as a site for awaiting further evacuation.

I was still there when the rescue pilot was found, just barely alive. They put him in a room not far from mine. While he was housed with us at the station, we all kept our mouths shut and tried to act normal. I felt enormously sorry for him and eventually understood the horrible alternatives he faced. I could not hold it against him; it was the law of the Arctic.

Of equal fascination to me is the incredible history of the region. Sir John Franklin (1786–1847) of the British Royal Navy disappeared on his last expedition attempting to chart and navigate the Northwest Passage with two ships, the Terror and the Erebus. The ships were caught in a storm and became trapped in ice for several years near Prince of Wales Island. Many succumbed to disease, and Franklin finally decided their only hope was to walk to southern Canada.

Only several decades later were their bodies found a hundred miles away. Being good Englishmen, among the supplies they dragged with them were all their dress uniforms and their fine china and cutlery. Evidence suggests that they, too, resorted to cannibalism to survive, but ultimately all died from exposure. Their two ships were finally discovered two centuries later, frozen solid in the ice, in 2014 and 2016.

Historically, the original explorers treated the very scant native population with haughty disregard. It is now readily accepted that if it hadn't been for that arrogant attitude toward the natives by the explorers, many more would have survived. In fact, in the course of one of his travels, the famous explorer Alexander

Mackenzie thought he was on his deathbed in a small hut his team had built for emergency survival. He had arrived there alone, the sole survivor of his expedition. As he lay there, breathing what he was sure was his last breath, there was a knock on the door and in walked a native. The surprise must have been mutually enormous. The native saved Mackenzie's life.

By the time I began visiting the Arctic, native populations resided in their own communities and sometimes worked as casual labor for foreigners. Relations between natives and newcomers appeared friendly, and I recall that we made an effort to help and work with these small groups of native people.

Visiting these extremely remote and historic locations gave me the chills, especially when thinking about what the early explorers must have gone through. On one occasion touring DEW Line stations, we landed on a remote beach. We joked and teased our British colleagues when staff members from the British contingent appeared and proceeded to set a table with forks and knives for our picnic. Things hadn't changed!

Having explored the North Pole, how could I go on without at least visiting the other end of the world? It, too, held a fascination. My wife and I took a trip to Antarctica in 2004, sailing on the 110-passenger ship the Endeavor. The South Pole greeted us with huge icebergs all over, distant mountains, and vast plains of ice and snow. It seemed much more civilized than the Arctic: lots of people (relatively, of course) and large animal populations. One everlasting memory for me is the huge fields of penguins and flocks of birds—albatrosses, hawks, cormorants, eagles, and others. Whole animal cultures survive in these barren lands, including sea lions, walruses, and whales.

We actually witnessed a leopard sea lion hunt and eat its prey: It sneaked up on a penguin, leapt on it to grab its throat, then, with a vicious toss of its head, killed the animal. The sea lion chewed a bit on the carcass, then took the body in its jaws and violently shook it until the flesh came flying out of its skin. Voilà, dinner was served.

We also found a greater variety of human settlements—stations belonging to America, Norway, Russia, Sweden, Poland, Greenland, Canada, and Finland. Compared to the Arctic, where nations clearly claim contiguous land, the land in Antarctica is not owned by any one nation, which creates more international competition.

The trip was thoroughly enjoyable and educational, with stops at research stations, abandoned early explorer camps, and the site where Robert F. Scott established his base as he sought to be the first to reach the South Pole. He apparently reached the Pole a scant few days after the Norwegian explorer Roald Amundsen. To his enormous disappointment, he found Amundsen's marker already there. On the trip back to his base camp, he and his team ran into really bad weather. He ended up with only three or four survivors in one tent where they huddled together waiting for a break in the storm.

Scott kept a diary and reported that at one moment, one of the four quietly hoisted himself to his feet and announced he was going to step outside for a second. He closed the tent flap behind him and was not seen again. Scott's diary reports the event very briefly. A few days later, when the weather did lift and search parties went looking for the team, they came across the tent with its frozen inhabitants. The last body was found not far from the tent, under a snowbank.

Apparently tourism in Antarctica has become a real problem. Ever larger cruise vessels, some with hundreds if not thousands of tourists, pour out of their ships onto the fragile landscape. In a side attraction for the hardier tourists, ships drop anchor in shallow bays during the summer so passengers can take a quick dip in the ocean (presumably so that they can say they did it). My understanding is that successful efforts are being made to limit tourism, which has really become a threat to the environment.

Even more ominous is the fact that global warming is melting ice so rapidly that the Arctic regions are ever more accessible. Tour ships are already advertising circumnavigating North America.

In my humble opinion, outsiders entering this very fragile part of the world should be highly regulated. It is naïve to think a campground built by explorers a hundred years ago will remain chaste if hordes of tourists armed with cameras descend upon it, unless there are strict controls.

I think of myself as having been so fortunate to have glimpsed the area at a time when things were only beginning to change. I have nothing but admiration for the local native inhabitants who adapted and survived, thrived, and actually created a remarkable culture of their own under the direst of circumstances. The earliest explorers, who found themselves struggling to survive, showed incredible toughness. Their greatest impediment may have been not the environment but their cultural inhibitions and reluctance to engage with the native population.

Although no longer sailing my own boat or piloting my own plane, my love of adventure tourism persists. For my eightieth birthday, in 2013, I thought it would be fun for the family to visit the famous Amazon River basin, particularly the upper reaches, much of which are relatively undeveloped. Indigenous tribes still live along its banks, and a little further inland there still exist some truly isolated native habitations.

We signed up for a boat trip on a stretch of river still not too developed for tourist traffic. The flat-bottomed vessel carried about thirty passengers quite comfortably. Our guides took us up the river, eventually tying up to overhanging trees, then onto motorized canoes along increasingly narrow and shallow streams that flowed into the parent river. We saw occasional wild animals—sloths and caimans, a variety of monkeys, countless birds, fish, and aquatic life, including many piranhas. Snakes, tarantulas, and a wide variety of extremely poisonous frogs were present, too, and one always had to be careful where one walked.

A bit unnerving was the presence of armed policemen on each boat. We were told this was to discourage bandits from sneaking on board at night, while we were tied up to the trees, and robbing the passengers. The thieves would be long gone back in the jungle before any effective outside help could be summoned, so armed policemen were *de rigueur*.

We went swimming in the river at one point after being reassured we were in a piranha-free stretch. The river regularly changed color, usually from a ruddy brown to a pitch black. They stopped the boat and told us we could swim when we hit a particularly large chunk of black water. The fish apparently can't tolerate the black water and stay well clear of it. In we went, and it was true. Trust the natives; they know whereof they speak.

It was an unforgettable trip into a different world. The sheer beauty and vastness of the ever-present jungle towering above us, the sounds of animals and birds, the peace and tranquility, the beauty of the vegetation, unspoiled by humans, and the meandering river and its tributaries were just incredible.

I was the only casualty. A large local ant thought I looked tasty. Wow, did that bite hurt! The locals immediately put some native salve on the bite, and, in not too many minutes, the pain subsided. For a brief while, I was sure I was a goner despite reassurances (and probably some discreet local chuckles) that it was "just" a local ant bite.

On this trip I saw that one of my passions has definitely been passed on to the next generations. My kids and grandkids enjoy our family trips as much now as when they were younger. This travel legacy, for lack of a better word, has been wonderful for all of us.

We have shared so many unique experiences that bind us together. The love of travel, the adventure of going to new places and immersing ourselves in foreign cultures and customs is important to the whole family. The oldest grandkids already look forward to traveling on their own.

Acknowledgments

This book would never have seen the light of day if it weren't for so many friends, family, business partners, and skilled individuals who were ready to contribute to the cause.

First and foremost must be Jane Constantineau, our priceless editor. Next, this book would be nothing without my gang of creative geniuses—those who actually did the work:

Paul Doherty, George Proctor, Mike Dow, John Arnold, Gary Cunningham, Douglas Hartley, George S.K. Rider, William (Billy) Ming Sing Lee, Steve Young, and my very supportive and talented Swiss cousins, Robert Nef, Maja Nef, and Erica Kuster-Nef. Thanks to Barbara Nef, who helped coordinate her gifted siblings to join our book project.

My long-time friends and The Ed Nef Foundation Board Members Ed Story and Bill Fitzhugh have been extremely supportive to nearly all my projects, including this book.

Meiyue Zhou, my loyal and indefatigable executive director, always responded quickly and wisely to every occasion with good humor and great patience. Damon Chung, my long-time

IT manager and cinematographer, was very helpful in setting up a new section about my book projects on the Ed Nef and family website and social media.

About Ed Nef

Born in New York City to a Swiss father and a Polish mother, Ed Nef grew up immersed in multiple languages and cultures. After a two-year detour to Stuttgart, Germany, with the US Army, Ed entered the US Foreign Service in 1959.

Starting in Dakar, Senegal, as an economic officer, his assignments took him to Guatemala, Colombia, and Canada. Breaking up his State Department tours were two stints with the new US Peace Corps. In 1976, Ed won a State Department Congressional Fellowship to work on Capitol Hill, which led to a permanent position as legislative director for Senator Max Baucus of Montana.

A career in the rigid and bureaucratic State Department and years in the hectic world of politics left Ed wanting to create something of his own. He found a promising opportunity in the "businesses for sale" section of *The Washington Post*: a foreign language school. Ed bought the school and turned it into the largest independent language school in the Washington, DC area. Eventually, Ed opened English language schools in Japan, Mongolia, and Vietnam.

His fascination with the countries he visited—and a knack for the visual arts—led him into the world of documentary film production. He produced films on topics ranging from the postwar relationship between the US and Vietnam to the rights of women in Senegal and the mining industry in Mongolia.

In one last great adventure, Ed began a family foundation, The Ed Nef Foundation, to support worthy projects around the world. His most recent effort was providing prosthetics to seriously disabled Mongolian individuals.

In the midst of his eclectic professional life, Ed managed to squeeze in another half a career as a flight instructor. Today, he lives with his wife, Elizabeth, in Northern Virginia. They have three daughters and four grandchildren.

Ed will be publishing e-book and audiobook editions of this title. He is also the author of a memoir, *Life Out Loud: A Memoir of Countless Adventures and No Regrets*, published in 2020. For more information, visit www.ednef.com.

The Nef family boating on the Peruvian Amazon.

CPSIA information can be obtained
at www.ICGtesting.com
Printed in the USA
LVHW092356120820
662878LV00013B/238

9 781734 171624